ARCTIC OCEAN

Petrograd (St. Petersburg)

RUSSIA

SIBERIA

MONGOLIA

MANCHURIA

Mukden

KOREA

CHINA

JAPAN

PACIFIC OCEAN

TURKEY

CYPRUS

Damascus

Jerusalem

Cairo

Gaza

Aqaba

PERSIA

AFGHANISTAN

TIBET

NEPAL BHUTAN

INDIA

BURMA

Tsingtao

HONG KONG (BR)

MARIANA ISLANDS (GER)

MARSHALL ISLANDS (GER)

EGYPT

SUDAN

ADEN

FRENCH SOMALILAND

BRITISH SOMALILAND

ABYSSINIA

BRITISH EAST AFRICA

ITALIAN SOMALILAND

SIAM

FRENCH INDO-CHINA

ANDAMAN ISLANDS (BR)

CEYLON

PHILIPPINE ISLANDS

PALAU ISLANDS (GER)

CAROLINE ISLANDS (GER)

MALAY STATES

SINGAPORE (BR)

BORNEO

GIAN NGO

Lake nganyika

GERMAN EAST AFRICA

Tanga

Dar es Salaam

thville

N. RHODESIA

MOZAMBIQUE

MADAGASCAR

DUTCH EAST INDIES

BISMARCK ARCHIPELAGO (GER)

GERMAN NEW GUINEA

BRITISH NEW GUINEA

SOLOMON ISLANDS (BR)

NEW HEBRIDES (FR & BR)

FIJI ISLANDS (BR)

SAMOA

NEW CALEDONIA (FR)

INDIAN OCEAN

CHRISTMAS ISLAND (BR)

COCOS ISLANDS (BR)

MAURITIUS (BR)

REUNION (FR)

OUTH RICA

AUSTRALIA

KERMADEC ISLANDS (BR)

Sydney

Auckland

NEW ZEALAND

N

W

E

S

AN INCOMPLETE HISTORY OF WORLD WAR I

PIER **9**

AN
INCOMPLETE HISTORY
OF
WORLD WAR I

EDWIN KIESTER JR

First published in 2007 by Pier 9, an imprint of Murdoch Books Pty Limited

Murdoch Books Australia
Pier 8/9
23 Hickson Road
Millers Point NSW 2000
Phone: +61 (0)2 8220 2000
Fax: +61 (0)2 8220 2558
www.murdochbooks.com.au

Murdoch Books UK Limited
Erico House
6th Floor
93–99 Upper Richmond Road
Putney, London SW15 2TG
Phone: +44 (0) 20 8785 5995
Fax: +44 (0) 20 8785 5985

Chief Executive: Juliet Rogers
Publishing Director: Kay Scarlett

Publisher: William Kiester
Design Concept: Sarah Odgers
Designer: Cathy Campbell
Project Manager: Emma Hutchinson
Editor: Scott Forbes
Photo Researchers: Amanda McKittrick and Catherine Taylor
Peer review: Peter Dean
Cartographer: Ian F Faulkner & Associates
Production: Adele Troeger

National Library of Australia Cataloguing-in-Publication Data
Kiester, Edwin, Jr.
        An incomplete history of World War I.
        Bibliography.
        Includes index.
        ISBN 978 1 74045 970 9.
        ISBN 1 74045 970 9.
        1. World War, 1914-1918 - History. I. Title. (Series : An
        incomplete history ; 1).
        940.3
Printed by C & C Offset Printing Co. Ltd in 2007. PRINTED IN CHINA.
Reprinted 2007.

In memory of
Edwin Hammitt Kiester Sr.,
Corporal, U.S. Army Signal Corps,
1914-1918,
and Lilla Marion Plowden,
whom he met and married,
Camp Sevier, South Carolina,
Thanksgiving 1918

CONTENTS

A soldier takes cover in the remnants of Château Wood near Ypres, in November 1917.

INTRODUCTION

'Some damn foolish thing in the Balkans', German chancellor Otto von Bismarck had said, would likely trigger the next great war in Europe. In 1914, that 'damn foolish thing' was the assassination of an Austrian archduke. The resulting cataclysm enveloped all of Europe and much of the world for four years and three months. On one side of the conflict were the Central Powers: Austria-Hungary, Germany, Bulgaria and Turkey. On the other, the Allies: France, Britain (along with its dominions of Australia, New Zealand, Canada and South Africa), Russia, Japan, later the United States, and a host of smaller states. Germany commenced hostilities by simultaneously attacking France in the west and Russia in the east. On the western front in particular, fighting quickly devolved into a stalemate of slogging, bitter trench warfare, punctuated by a few major battles claiming hundreds of thousands of lives. The war soon spread to the air and the sea, and to Africa, the Middle East, Asia and even the South Pacific. In addition to the armies of the European powers, it involved colonial troops from India, North Africa and the Middle East. By the time it ended, sixty million men had been under arms, three emperors had been dethroned and a communist regime had been installed in Russia. The Armistice of 11 November 1918, represented not so much victory or defeat, but sheer exhaustion.

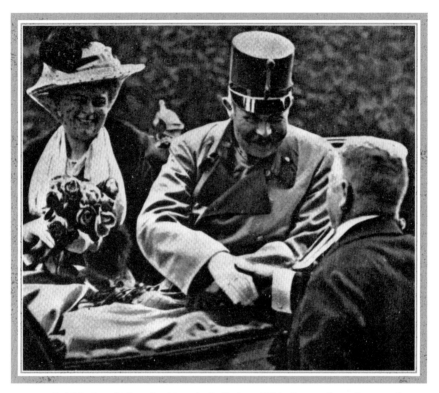

Archduke Franz Ferdinand and his wife, the Duchess of Hohenberg, on June 28 1914, in Sarajevo

At the beginning of 1914, there hadn't been a war involving all the major European powers for almost a century, since Napoleon's defeat at Waterloo in 1815. But the recent economic and political growth of Germany and the emergence of a unified Italy had made the traditional powers nervous. France sought an ally and found one in Russia. Britain, protected by the sea and its navy, followed a policy of 'splendid isolation', but meanwhile negotiated an entente cordiale, or 'friendly understanding', with France and, consequently, Russia, an agreement that became known as the 'Triple Entente'. In response, Germany struck a 'Triple Alliance' with Austria-Hungary and Italy. Thus, while Europe was technically at peace, it was in reality divided into rival camps, both primed for war.

CHAPTER ONE

TWO BULLETS THAT LED TO NINE MILLION DEATHS

THE ASSASSINATION OF ARCHDUKE FRANZ FERDINAND

Suddenly, startlingly, the open car veered round the corner and screeched to a halt, right in front of him. In the rear seat, less than two metres away, sat the heir to the throne of Austria-Hungary, Archduke Franz Ferdinand, resplendent in his gold-braided uniform and gilt-trimmed helmet, and his wife, the Duchess of Hohenberg, smiling under a wide-brimmed hat and veil. She was holding the archduke's hand.

The thin, spidery youth with the piercing black eyes had fired the Browning pistol only once before, in an impromptu target practice, and missed with almost half his shots. This time, however, his aim was true. The first bullet caught the archduke in the throat, pitching him forwards into his wife's lap. 'In God's name, what is happening to you?' she cried, before a second bullet struck her in the abdomen. 'Sopherl! Sopherl! Don't die! Stay alive for the children!' onlookers heard the archduke cry, using his pet name for the duchess. But the duchess, too, collapsed, and before either could receive medical attention, the royal couple had bled to death.

Swinging their sabres, horrified officers from the royal entourage knocked the young man to the ground and wrestled away his pistol. Spectators piled on top, pinning him down. The struggling prisoner somehow managed to pull a cyanide pill from his pocket and force it into his mouth, only to regurgitate it seconds later.

There was no chance of escape, but, buried beneath the pile of bodies, Gavrilo Princip felt nothing but satisfaction. He and his co-conspirators, a motley crew of students and misfits, had struck a blow for their beloved cause—the creation of a Greater Serbia. Little did they realise that the two shots that had just echoed down the quay, on this day of 28 June 28 1914, in Sarajevo, Bosnia, would be the first in a conflagration that would engulf all Europe and cost nine million lives.

A SYMBOL OF OPPRESSION

It had never occurred to the plotters that the assassination might have 'serious consequences', one of Princip's fellow conspirators said later. He never would have taken part, he insisted, if he had known it would 'lead to a world war'. Indeed, only one of the almost farcical band of youthful assassins seems to have given the impact of their actions much thought. Danilo Ilic, oldest of the group at twenty-four, had repeatedly asked, 'But what will it accomplish?' They thought they were simply making a political statement while striking a blow against oppression.

Most of the group knew little about their target. But as the head of the Hapsburg Empire, the archduke was the personification of Austrian oppression of Bosnian Serbs. And that made him fair game. The Serbs had suffered centuries of foreign domination, beginning with their humiliating defeat at the hands of invading Turkish armies at the battle of Kosovo in 1389. Under the Ottoman Turks, Christian Orthodox Serbs were pushed into the most mountainous, marginal lands of the Balkan Peninsula. They continued to fight for their independence, however, and in the early 1800s they finally managed to throw off Turkish rule and establish their own monarchy, which was recognised by other countries in 1878.

But more than half a million Orthodox Serbs remained outside this state, in the provinces of Bosnia and Herzegovina, where they were nominally under Turkish rule but governed by the Hapsburgs of Catholic Austria-Hungary. When the Turkish empire finally began to collapse in the early years of the twentieth century, the Austrians simply annexed the largely Slavic provinces. Serbs everywhere were enraged by the 'theft', which, they charged, unjustifiably made 'slaves' of the Bosnian Serbs.

Princip knew the oppression and suffering of the Bosnian Serbs all too well. He had been born into a poor family of *kmets*, peasants who lived in a two-room hovel with a smoke hole in the roof. The family laboriously tilled a tiny, two-hectare plot of scruffy land in the Krajina, the most impoverished region of Bosnia. They were not allowed to own land and were forced to pay one-third of the cash value of their meagre crops to a landlord, usually a Muslim. To pay the debt and feed his family, Petar Princip, Gavrilo's father, was forced to deliver mail and operate a rickety transport service over the mountains, while his wife tended the fields.

'Gavro' was one of ten children, six of whom died in infancy. He grew up undersized and frail, and was bullied by peers and school-mates. To escape their taunts, Gavrilo turned to books. Bosnia was ninety per cent illiterate, but he became the first member of his family to read and write. 'Books were my life', he was to recall later. He immersed himself in epics of Serbian history, weeping over the tragic defeat at Kosovo and swearing to himself that he would take up arms for the cause of a united Serbia.

THIS GUN FOR HIRE

Assassination had become a favoured form of political protest in the late 1800s and early 1900s. Four kings, three American presidents, the Empress of Austria, two monarchical heirs and assorted dukes, barons, governors, legislators and other political figures had been gunned down or stabbed to death by 1911. The King of Serbia died in a grisly 1903 massacre in which he, the queen and her two brothers were shot and then thrown out of palace windows. The estranged wife of Hapsburg Emperor Franz Josef, Elisabeth of Bavaria, was stabbed to death by an anarchist in Geneva in 1898. That these assassinations seemed to change little did not decrease their popularity.

While Princip was in school in 1911, a fellow student, Bogdan Zerajic, fired four shots at the Austro-Hungarian governor of Bosnia. He missed, and used his last bullet to shoot himself. Others ridiculed him as an impetuous schoolboy and a blundering fool. But not Princip. He saw Zerajic as a hero, a martyr to the Serbian cause, and he took a vow at Zerajic's graveside to follow in the young man's footsteps.

Gavrilo Princip in jail awaiting trial

As a first step, Princip moved to Belgrade in 1913 to further his education. At the time, inspired by events in Russia, all of Europe was in revolutionary ferment. Radical parties in France and Germany were flexing their muscles. In the Balkans, Croats, Slovenes and Muslims, as well as Serbs, were agitating for freedom from Hapsburg rule. Cries went up for a union of all southern Slavs in a single country, to be called Yugoslavia. Belgrade was a hotbed of revolutionary fervour. Princip was by now reading and soaking up the teachings of the Russian anarchists, particularly those of Peter Alekseyevich Kropotkin, an advocate of the use of tyrannicide—the killing of an unjust ruler—to liberate oppressed people. He began to frequent a cheap café, the Green Garland, where hotheaded young men gathered nightly over coffee and powerful plum brandy to argue politics far into the night. There was much talk of violence as the only plausible route to advance Serbian causes. 'History moves too slowly', one agitator shouted. 'It needs a push!'

Secret societies to provide that push were forming on both sides of the border. In Sarajevo, a group calling itself Young Bosnia announced its goal as 'the unification of Serbdom' by 'all means available'. In Belgrade, a group named Norodna Obranda enrolled nearly 5,000 members and called for forcible action to overturn the Austro-Hungarian annexation of Bosnia and Herzegovina. Under pressure from the Serbian government, it subsequently renounced violence and re-formed as a cultural society. But a breakaway group calling itself Union or Death, and known to its enemies as the Black Hand, was founded by a colonel in Serbian army intelligence—one of the officers who had led the attack on the Serbian king in 1903. Its 2,500 members, organised into cells of between three and five people, pledged to uphold the goals of 'terrorist action', as opposed to 'intellectual propaganda', and to infiltrate other organisations.

Princip was not a born conspirator. He was a teetotaller and a loner who led an almost monastic life. In the cafés, he avoided the plum brandy, sipped only water and took little part in the discussions. 'I was not in general gifted as a talker', he was to say later to a psychiatrist who examined him in prison. 'I was always a reader and always alone, not often engaging in debates.' But he listened intently to the others' arguments, and the terrorists' words convinced him. Violence was the only answer. Someone had to strike a fatal blow—and right at the heart of Austrian power.

Then fifty-year-old Archduke Franz Ferdinand wasn't yet the official ruler of Austria-Hungary, and wouldn't ascend the imperial throne until his eighty-three-year-old uncle, Franz Josef, passed away. He was, in reality, sympathetic to Slav aspirations—his wife, indeed, was a Slav (specifically, a Czech)—and he had advanced the idea of a three-pronged monarchy, under which the empire's Slavic subjects would be given equality with Austrians and Hungarians. Serbs, however, viewed this unfavourably, believing it would only end their dream of a united Serbia. Moreover, Princip had convinced himself that the archduke wielded a malign influence at the royal court against the Slavs.

Princip decided he must assassinate Franz Ferdinand.

ONE HOUR OF BAD PRACTICE

Princip realised, however, that he needed collaborators. He shared his Belgrade room with another rebellious young Bosnian, eighteen-year-old Trifko Grabez, who had been expelled from school and jailed in Sarajevo for assaulting a professor in a political argument. When his friend confided his dream of assassination, Grabez, thirsty for revenge on authority, immediately agreed to participate.

In February 1914, the teenagers read in a newspaper that Archduke Franz Ferdinand, as inspector general of the Austro-Hungarian forces, would come to Bosnia on 28 June to observe army manoeuvres. Whether anyone in the Austro-Hungarian administration realised it or not, it was a provocative choice of day: 28 June was the anniversary of the battle of Kosovo. For Princip, it was an obvious opportunity for a symbolic act.

Princip recruited Nedjelko Cabrinovic, another Bosnian, whom he considered his best friend in Belgrade, and an old friend in Sarajevo, Danilo Ilic. Princip wrote to Ilic, urging him to locate three more volunteers and said he would arrive in Sarajevo in May, bringing guns and bombs. He failed to mention certain impediments, however: none of the conspirators had access to guns or bombs, or had money to buy them, and none had ever held a gun, let alone fired one.

Despite this, Princip persevered and managed to make contact with a former Serbian guerilla leader and, through him, with Dragutin Dimitrijevic, a Serbian intelligence officer and then leader of the Black Hand. Soon, he took delivery of four Browning pistols—each loaded with eight cartridges—reserve ammunition, six bombs filled with nails and bits of lead, plus a supply of cyanide. Also in the package were instructions on how to use the bombs: 'unscrew the cap, knock the bomb against something hard, count three, throw the bomb, then wait ten to thirteen seconds for the explosion'. The untrained would-be killers were given one hour's pistol instruction and target practice in a nearby forest.

WELCOMING THE ARCHDUKE

Sunday 28 June 1914 was to be a banner day in Sarajevo. The archduke's visit was to be brief, but ceremonial. He would spend 26 and 27 June watching military manoeuvres. The next day he would be joined by his wife, and the two would travel in a slow, seven-car motorcade six kilometres along the quay to the town hall. There would be speeches and welcomes and then the motorcade would proceed through the narrow streets adorned with the yellow-and-black double-eagle imperial banner to the new museum, which the archduke would dedicate. A grand lunch would follow, after which the royal couple would depart for Vienna.

Princip learned of the archduke's exact schedule only a few days before the visit. On the night of 27 June, he called a meeting of the conspirators in a café garden to draw up the final plans, issue guns, bombs and cyanide capsules, and meet the new accomplices. Ilic had recruited two schoolboys, seventeen-year-old Vaso Cubrilovic and eighteen-year-old Cvjetko Popovic, as well as Muhamed Mehmedbasic,

FRANZ AND SOPHIE: A LOVE STORY

Franz Ferdinand dearly loved his wife Sophie, but few others did in the snooty imperial household. After all, she was a mere countess, not of royal blood, and a Slav at that. Emperor Franz Josef permitted their marriage only on condition that it were morganatic—their children would never have rights to the throne, Sophie could not become queen, and in royal protocol she had to be grouped with the other, lesser nobles. Sarajevo was a rare chance for them to appear together proudly, since the archduke was appearing as a military commander, not a royal personage; 28 June was also a day for personal celebration as it was their wedding anniversary.

They died holding hands.

Even in death, the court could not accept the archduke's wife. As a mere countess, she was not permitted to have a state funeral, and her coffin was not allowed in the archduke's cortege. Nor could she be interred in the Hapsburg royal crypt, for that, it was said, would defile the monarchy.

In the end, the archduke and his beloved Sophie were entombed side by side, at their country home, just as Franz Ferdinand had requested.

twenty-seven, a Muslim carpenter who claimed to have once attempted to assassinate the Austro-Hungarian military commander Oskar Potiorek.

Princip and Grabez had concluded that the best place for an ambush would be along the six-kilometre motorcade route. The archduke would be too well guarded at the railway station, the town hall, and the castle outside Sarajevo where he and his wife would be staying overnight. The slow motorcade would allow for a more accurate gunshot or throw of a bomb.

Princip decided that the conspirators would be posted about thirty metres apart. He gave guns to the two youngest recruits, Cubrilovic and Popovic, and to Grabez, keeping the fourth for himself. He issued a bomb to each man with instructions to conceal it under his coat, and divided the cyanide into six packets. Then Grabez, Ilic and Princip went to a café, where Princip, uncharacteristically, toasted the success of their enterprise with a glass of wine, swallowed in a gulp.

Next morning, all were at their appointed stations, sweating in dark suits or heavy clothes that were worn to conceal the bombs, but that also, on this muggy day, drew quizzical looks from bystanders. Mehmedbasic was first in line as the motorcade proceeded up the quay, but he merely watched it go by and left his bomb untouched. The youthful Cubrilovic followed his example: 'When I saw the archduke, I could not bring myself to kill him', he said later.

Cabrinovic, next in line, was cooler. 'Which is the archduke's car?' he asked a police guard. 'The third one', the helpful guard replied. Whereupon Cabrinovic took out his bomb, rapped it against a tramway sign to release the safety cap and aimed it directly at the archduke. It missed him by centimetres, bouncing off the car into the street and exploding in front of the next car; one guard was hurt and taken to hospital. Cabrinovic, who had not been trusted with a gun, tried to swallow his cyanide capsule but spilled most of it. With a bound, he leapt over a fence and dived into the Miljacka River, which, however, was less than a metre deep. He was then captured easily by police. 'Who are you?' a policeman asked. 'I am a Serbian hero', Cabrinovic said proudly.

The archduke insisted that they halt the procession as soon as the car could safely stop to see if anyone had been seriously injured. That brought him in front of Princip, but because of his short stature the would-be assassin could not see over the other onlookers and had no field of fire. By the time he was able to wriggle through the crowd, the procession had moved on.

But half an hour later the cars came back down the quay at high speed, passing a surprised Grabez, who had no time to react, and the archduke's driver made the wrong turn that would bring him to a final rendezvous with Princip—and death.

THE TALKATIVE CONSPIRATOR

In prison, Cabrinovic disclosed names and details of the plot, partly at Princip's urging. Police had rounded up more than two hundred Serbs, and Serb homes and businesses had been burned down and demolished. 'Tell everything so that just people do not come to harm', Princip told Grabez. Mehmedbasic escaped to Montenegro, but the other conspirators were soon caught.

Under Austrian law, anyone aged eighteen and under could not be executed. Princip, Cabrinovic and Grabez received the maximum twenty years' imprisonment, Cubrilovic and Popovic sixteen and thirteen years, respectively. Ilic, being slightly older, was sentenced to hang along with two other men who had helped smuggle the weapons into Bosnia and two peasants who had assisted along the way, but their sentences were later commuted to life imprisonment. By that time the Austrians and the tenacious Serbs were clashing along the border, the Germans were closing in on Paris and thousands of men had already died across Europe.

Kaiser Wilhelm II and General Helmuth von Moltke inspecting German troops in 1914

The assassination of Franz Ferdinand offered Austria-Hungary an opportunity to punish the upstart Serbians. But Serbia had long been supported by Russia, and although Austria thought Russia unlikely to intervene in any subsequent conflict, it sought German backing for its actions. Consulted on 5 July, Kaiser Wilhelm pledged his 'faithful support', later described as a blank cheque. Reassured, Austria sent a fifteen-page ultimatum to the Serbian government on 23 July, fully expecting it to be rejected. Blaming Serbian military intelligence for plotting the assassination, Austria demanded that Serbia condemn the alleged military involvement, ban anti-Hapsburg propaganda, cease interfering in Bosnia and agree to a joint Austrian-Serbian investigation of the assassination. Serbia was given forty-eight hours to comply—or else. As the crisis escalated, frantic, high-level diplomatic manoeuvring began.

WHO PUT OUT THE LIGHTS?

SIR EDWARD GREY'S DIPLOMATIC CRISIS

The summer of 1914 was the most glorious anyone in Europe could remember, and everyone who could afford it went off on holiday. The British royal family retreated to its summer palace. Half the ambassadors of the major European nations went on leave. On 6 July, having reassured Austria-Hungary of his support, Kaiser Wilhelm embarked on a three-week cruise in Norwegian waters. The czar retreated to his beach house on the Baltic. And every weekend of the month, as he usually did, the British foreign secretary, Sir Edward Grey, went fly-fishing in Scotland.

There were few troublesome diplomatic affairs for the foreign secretary to deal with immediately, anyway. 'The German government are in a very peaceful mood and very anxious to be on good terms with England', he had said the month before of Britain's burgeoning arch-rival for naval and economic supremacy. True, there was a little trouble in Bosnia—the assassination of the heir to the Hapsburg throne—but there was always unrest in the Balkans, nothing that couldn't be handled. Seeking the wily trout in the rippling lakes and streams of the Highlands in the soft summer morning light was an invitation not to be refused.

Fishing and listening to bird calls were the chief passions of the foreign secretary, a solitary, buttoned-up man who was the very epitome of the cautious diplomat. A childless widower, then aged fifty-two, Grey was hardly your prototypical political figure. Although he had been in Parliament for twenty-nine years and foreign secretary for more than eight, he was not at all a gregarious handshaker, and on weekends could scarcely escape to the countryside quickly enough. In parliamentary questioning he was laconic, evasive and could seldom be trapped into a clear, definite answer on any subject, always carefully and cautiously declining to commit himself, always leaving himself an out. He had a 'walled personality', an associate said.

That caution and that reserve were to play a crucial role—some would say the crucial role—in the events leading up to the Great War.

THE MOST FORMIDABLE DOCUMENT EVER SENT

When Austria-Hungary delivered its ultimatum to Belgrade, all of Europe was stunned by its vehemence, its accusations and its demands, Grey included. It was 'the most formidable document ever sent from one state to another', he said. Still, the dispute seemed to him just another of those nasty quarrels in the far-off Balkans. 'If it did not lead to trouble between Austria and Russia, I had no concern with it', he declared. In any case, Britain's attention was focused nearer home; forces in Ulster, the northernmost and mainly Protestant portion of Ireland, were threatening outright rebellion against Home Rule.

On 26 July, supported by Russia, Serbia rejected Austria's ultimatum; although agreeing to most of Austria's demands, the refusal took particular exception to allowing Austrian participation in the investigation and trial of the assassins. That would violate the Serbian constitution, it was said. Thus, on Tuesday, 28 July, one month to the day after Franz Ferdinand's murder, Austria declared war on Serbia. The next day, Austria shelled Belgrade. Now, as one German diplomat said, 'the iron dice had been rolled'.

While still hoping the fuss could be confined to a minor-league to-do in the Balkans, the two sides began to line up. Russia backed Serbia, and France assured Russia of its support. Austria and Germany, the Central Powers, stood side by side; Italy, though allied to Germany and Austria, opted to remain neutral.

With full-scale war impending in the last week of July, both sides pressed Grey to learn where Britain stood. Germany wanted Britain to adopt a hands-off policy and remain neutral. France hoped that if and when the crunch came, it could count on Britain for support. Grey was cordial but not willing to be pinned down, offering vague statements that both sides interpreted in their favour. He did, however, let it be known that 'it would be disagreeable to us' if Germany became the dominant power in continental Europe and the French ports on the English Channel fell into German hands. When British and French general staffs met to discuss possible military coordination in a hypothetical war, Grey approved their plan, but, in what the historian Barbara Tuchman called 'a masterpiece of ellipsis,' declared that it didn't really commit Britain to anything. In a letter to the French ambassador to Great Britain, Paul Cambon, Grey wrote that the talks left both Britain and France free to decide 'at any future time whether or not to assist each other with armed force'; in the event of a war threat, both sides 'would take into consideration' the staff talks and 'then decide what effect should be given them'.

Likewise, the British navy had agreed with France that in the event of war Britain would protect the French and Belgian ports on the Channel, which were important for British shipping, thus freeing the French fleet for operations elsewhere. But that didn't constitute a commitment in case of war, Grey said. It was a commitment to noncommitment.

Persuading Britain to remain neutral was the cornerstone of German policy. At a naval conference of 1912 meant to quell the naval arms race and establish the size of British and German high-seas fleets, Germany had agreed to a lesser fleet with the tacit understanding that Britain and its warships would remain neutral if war came. That would have tied Britain's hands, however, so Grey later persuaded King George V to state that it was British policy to keep all options open.

LET'S ALL TALK ABOUT IT

During the last few days of July, the telegraph wires between the Foreign Office and its counterparts in Paris and Berlin hummed constantly, while ambassadors in every capital exchanged frantic telephone messages or paid hurry-up visits to foreign embassies. On 26 July, Grey proposed an international conference of 'disinterested' parties to mediate in the dispute between Austria and Serbia. He suggested that ambassadors from Germany, France, Italy and Britain meet with him in London under Foreign Office auspices to forge a solution. At the very least, Grey said, the conference would buy time to arrange a settlement between the parties.

France and Italy immediately accepted. Germany said the real dispute lay between Austria and Serbia's ally Russia, which was already beginning to mobilise parts of its army on the Austrian frontier. Austria refused to abide by the conference's recommendations. All right, Grey said, falling back on his time-tested technique of opacity, let us have 'conversations' and 'friendly advice', informal meetings to determine what 'suggestions' could be made for settlement of the dispute.

But by 29 July, Austria had already captured Serbian territory. Grey persisted in his efforts to talk things down. He suggested that direct Austria-Russia talks continue; barring that, the four-power conference could convene. Meanwhile, Austria should halt its advance into Serbia but would be allowed to maintain the positions won and actually submit its demands from Serbian soil. At the same time, that territory would have to be relinquished after an agreement was reached, Grey said, because Serbian sovereignty and independence must not be impaired.

But with Russia threatening the Austrian frontier, Germany asserted that it had no choice but to mobilise, too. In response, Russia declared full mobilisation against both Austria and Germany. On 31 July, Germany gave Russia a twelve-hour ultimatum to demobilise. When the ultimatum expired without reply, Germany declared war. That meant France was treaty-bound to join Russia. 'The sword has been forced into our hand', Kaiser Wilhelm claimed.

THE BELGIAN QUESTION

France and Germany now faced each other across their heavily fortified common frontier. For Germany, however, Belgium, with its vast, level plain, presented a more natural avenue into France. However, in 1839 Britain, France and Germany had drafted the Treaty of Paris, establishing the state of Belgium and guaranteeing it neutrality in perpetuity. If any state violated Belgium's neutrality, the other signatories were obligated to come to Belgium's defence.

What would Britain do if Germany advanced through Belgium? Prince Karl-Max Lichnowsky, German ambassador to Britain, put that question to Grey by telephone on 31 July. Rather than answer directly, Grey cited the treaty 'to which we are both signatories'. However, he reminded Lichnowsky, Britain's policy was one of keeping options open. Lichnowsky then asked Grey what would happen if France were to strike first, crossing Belgian territory to thwart a German invasion. Grey was vague, again citing the treaty. Lichnowsky persevered. Suppose Germany were to invade only a small corner of Belgian territory, say, in the south-eastern Ardennes area, far from the capital and industrial centres? Grey would not be cornered, noting that the treaty did not make exceptions.

At the same time, Grey wired both France and Germany to ask for formal assurances that both countries would respect Belgian neutrality 'so long as no other power violates it'. France agreed within an hour; Germany did not answer.

Next day, Cambon called on Grey again. At this point Germany was massing troops on the Belgian border. Seeking to nullify any German excuse for war by claiming France had struck first, the French government instructed all troops to move back ten kilometers from the Belgian border to prevent any accidental incursions of Belgian territory. Violators were to be shot on sight. Recalling Grey's earlier comment that Britain must eventually be dragged into any continental war, Cambon queried whether Britain would honour the Treaty of Paris in the event of a German invasion through Belgium. Belgian neutrality 'might become a factor', Grey admitted. But, as he understood the treaty, Belgium would have to state that its neutrality had been violated and formally ask for assistance. Not until that request could Britain 'consider' stepping in. Cambon then asked flatly: would Britain wait until

Sir Edward Grey, British foreign secretary

THE COUSINS' WAR

Europe in 1914 was a formidable bastion of monarchy and several of the crowned heads were related through Britain's Queen Victoria, who borne nine children and forty grandchildren and spread them liberally around the royal families of Europe. Czar Nicholas II of Russia was the first cousin of Kaiser Wilhelm by marriage. Wilhelm's sister Sophie was queen of Greece. His cousin Marie was queen of Romania, cousin Margaret crown princess of Sweden, cousin Victoria queen of Spain. Wilhelm himself was the eldest son of Victoria's first-born daughter, the Princess Royal Victoria Adelaide, and therefore first cousin of British King George V.

Nicky, Willy and Georgie, as the family referred to them, had known each other from childhood. Queen Victoria had fostered the family's far-flung ties—partly for political reasons—and each summer flocks of relatives would gather at her palace. But after Austria declared war on Serbia, the royal cousins faced the prospect of war against each other. The day after that declaration, Czar Nicholas scrawled out a telegram to his first cousin. He wrote in English, their common language. 'Dear Willy', he began.

Diplomatic efforts to forestall war had proved fruitless. In Nicholas's view it was time for the heavy hitters to step in. 'I appeal to you to help me', he wrote to Wilhelm. 'An ignoble war has been declared against a weak country. To try and avoid such a calamity as a European war, I beg you in the name of our old friendship to do what you can to stop your allies from going too far.'

Willy, meanwhile, was sending his own telegram, which crossed with Nicky's. It, too, emphasised the family relationship in somewhat awkward English: 'With regard to the hearty and tender friendship which binds us both from long ago with

German troops had actually crossed the French border? Grey replied with classic indirection, 'France must make her own decision without reckoning on an assistance we are not now in a position to give'. He prepared to see Cambon out, the interview over. 'What are you waiting for?' he asked. 'I am waiting to see if the word "honour" has been erased from the English dictionary', Cambon replied.

firm ties, I am exerting my utmost influence to induce the Austrians to deal straightly to arrive at a satisfactory understanding with you ... Your very sincere and devoted friend and cousin.'

A few hours later he sent a second telegram which was more blunt: 'It would be quite impossible for Russia to remain a spectator of the Austro–Serbian conflict without involving Europe in the most horrible war she ever witnessed. I think a direct understanding between your government and Vienna possible and desirable.'

Over the next few days, ten more messages flew back and forth as the two cousins plucked the family heartstrings, endeavouring to block the war, turn it to their advantage, or at least emerge as the good guys, the seekers of peace.

Throughout the negotiations, the kaiser remained convinced that Britain would stay neutral if Germany attacked France. Earlier in the summer, his brother Prince Henry had asked King George V what Britain would do in the event of war between Germany and France. The king responded that he was sure Britain 'would do its best to stay out of a European war'. The kaiser took his cousin's words to mean what he wanted them to mean: Britain would stay on the sidelines. When advisers reported that Britain was girding itself for war, he dismissed the idea: 'I have the word of a king, and that's good enough for me', he said.

But by 4 August, when Germany invaded Belgium, it was too late for any kind of royal intercession. Willy, Nicky and Georgie never communicated with or saw each other again. Willy had the last word. 'To think that George and Nicky should have played me false!'

Grey had sound political reasons for his inaction. The British cabinet, Parliament and the British public were sharply divided on the question of war. There was a strong antiwar faction in Grey's own Liberal Party, and if Britain jumped into the war, at least half the cabinet ministers could be expected to resign. There was measured public sympathy for beleaguered France, more for 'poor little Belgium', as that nation was widely known, but little for fighting on the side of Russia, which the British generally regarded as an oppressive, anti-Semitic power. Moreover, Britain had historic ties with Germany. The royal family's lineage was German, and the British and Prussian armies had fought together against Napoleon.

ALERTING THE NAVY

On 1 August, the French head of state, President Raymond Poincaré, poignantly appealed to King George, declaring that his country was about to be crushed. The king responded sympathetically but, at Grey's behest, pointed again to Britain's long-term policy of noncommitment.

Prime Minister Herbert Asquith announced his full support for Grey's position, but not all cabinet members agreed. On 2 August, Winston Churchill, First Lord of the Admiralty, ordered the British fleet to war stations at Scapa Flow, off the Scottish Orkney Islands, ready to hold off any German attempt to move out into the North Sea or towards the English Channel.

Cambon pleaded with Grey once more on 3 August. Grey replied that some new development—an invasion of Belgium, in other words—'must be awaited'. Prince Lichnowsky called on Grey, too, that day and, although he had been previously exposed to Grey's murky rhetoric, completely misinterpreted the conversation. He euphorically but incorrectly wired Berlin that 'in case we did not attack France, Britain would remain neutral and guarantee French neutrality in the event of a German war against Russia'. The kaiser, who had always pinned his faith on British neutrality and considered Russia the primary enemy, was ecstatic. He ordered that the mobilisation be stopped and all armies be turned towards Russia. The general staff objected. 'It cannot be done', said Helmuth von Moltke, the chief of staff, and the kaiser reluctantly agreed. A new telegram then came from Lichnowsky. 'A positive proposal by England is not in prospect', he said sadly.

Still Grey dithered, until Germany solved his dilemma for him. On 2 August, Berlin had sent an ultimatum to Belgium demanding that German troops be allowed full passage across Belgian territory. All Belgian fortifications, railways and troops had to be surrendered to German forces. The Belgian government was given twelve hours to comply. On 3 August, Belgium's King Albert defied the German demands and ordered his tiny army to resist. That same day, Grey had one last meeting with Lichnowsky. Grey was to address the House of Commons that afternoon. Would he request a declaration of war? Lichnowsky asked. Typically, Grey answered as vaguely as possible. It would be a 'statement of conditions', he said. Was Belgium one of the conditions? Lichnowsky enquired. Grey did not answer. Then, gathering his notes, he went before the House of Commons.

THE ISSUE AND THE CHOICE

Sweltering even in his lightweight summer suit, Grey began to review the events of the previous days for a House of Commons in which every chair was taken. In a level, almost unemotional voice, he asked the House to approach the crisis from the point of view of 'British interests, British honour, British obligations'. He described the military 'conversations', the naval agreement, and the French-Russian alliance—'to which we are not party'. None of these, he said, bound Britain's hands. He seemed to be trying so hard to avoid the word 'war' that one member of the house exclaimed, 'By God, they are going to abandon Belgium!' But Grey expanded on the naval agreements:

> If the German fleet came down the Channel and bombarded and battered the undefended coast of France, we could not stand aside and see this going on practically within sight of our eyes, with our arms folded, looking on dispassionately, doing nothing!

As the House cheered, he went on:

> I ask the House from the point of view of British interests to consider what may be at stake. If France is beaten to her knees, if Belgium fell under some dominating force, then Holland, then Denmark ... If, in a crisis like this, we run away from these obligations of honour and interests as regards the Belgian treaty ... we should, I believe, sacrifice our respect and good name and reputation before the world and should not escape the most serious and grave economic consequences.

He put the 'issue and the choice' before the House and the reaction was overwhelming applause. Grey's clear and genuine belief in the need to defend British 'honour and interests' carried the day. His fellow Liberals were more pacifist than the opposition Conservatives, but even they were ready, with a few exceptions, to vote for the 'choice' of war.

Grey now prepared to give Germany an ultimatum. Yet, characteristically, he waited twenty-four hours to take that irrevocable step, perhaps hoping that the British Parliament's response would force the Germans to back down. Meanwhile, Berlin had notified Paris that, in view of German newspaper accounts of violations of German territory, 'the German empire considers itself in a state of war with France'.

The next morning, August 4, at about 8 a.m., German troops moved into Belgium, bombarding the fortress at Liège with a monster 420-millimetre gun. At 2 p.m., Grey finally told the German government that Britain felt bound to uphold the neutrality of Belgium and the treaty 'to which Germany is as much partner as ourselves'. If Britain did not receive a 'satisfactory reply' by midnight (11 p.m. London time), announcing that Germany would pull its invasion force back from Belgium, the British ambassador, Sir Edward Goschen, was authorised by his government to 'ask for passports', the euphemism for a formal notice of war.

Sir Edward presented the ultimatum right on schedule to German Chancellor Theobald von Bethmann Hollweg, and was dressed down in angry terms. Britain, said Bethmann Hollweg, was doing an 'unthinkable thing', making war on a 'kindred nation'—a reference to the ethnic and dynastic links between the countries. It was like striking a man from behind while he was fighting for his life against two assailants. 'And all this', he said, 'for just a word, "neutrality"! All for a scrap of paper!' Sir Edward was given his passports. That the two countries were officially at war was ratified by the British Parliament the next day.

On the evening after his speech, Grey stood at a window of his Whitehall office, looking down into the broad thoroughfare as the evening lamps were being lit, knowing that war was now inevitable. 'The lamps are going out all over Europe', he said memorably. 'We shall not see them lighted again in our lifetime.'

But there were those on both sides who said he had contributed to bringing on the four years of darkness that lay ahead. And even today, while some argue that men like Grey had no hope of averting the crisis once mobilisation had started, there are those who say that if he had been firmer, more resolute, if he had stated Britain's position more clearly, if he had offered Britain's support to France and told Germany that Britain would not stand idly by while an ally was threatened, if he had tried to convince the British government to intercede sooner and more forcefully, then the onset of war might have been sidetracked. Cooler heads, like his own, might have prevailed. Or at the very least, the war might have been confined to those troublesome countries in the Balkans, and millions of lives might have been spared.

Crowds watch German troops march into Brussels on 20 August 1914

The failure of the diplomatic negotiations and the subsequent German advance into Belgium on 4 August 1914 committed much of Europe to war. The leading powers had been preparing for such an eventuality for decades. Military service had long been compulsory in all major European countries except Britain. Senior military staff in each country had developed a range of contingency plans for diverse scenarios and foes, including mobilisation of civilian forces and transportation of troops, mainly by train. The plan that was to be carried out most diligently and was to have the greatest impact on the war was hatched in Berlin. Like the others, it had been in development for decades, but its origins stretched back to the days of the Roman Empire.

THE BEST-LAID PLANS

EACH SIDE'S STRATEGY FOR
A SPEEDY VICTORY

Count Alfred von Schlieffen was the epitome of the Prussian militarist. The son of a general, he was aloof and arrogant, observing his inferiors with a scowl and a monocle screwed into his right eye, and single-minded about war. It was said, for example, that he read military history as bedtime stories to his daughter. These were qualities that appealed to Kaiser Wilhelm II, who in 1891 named him chief of the German Great General Staff, even though he had never commanded a major army in the field and had seen combat only as a minor officer in Prussia's seven-week war against Austria in 1866 and in the Franco-Prussian War of 1870–71. Prior to his appointment, he had spent seven years as chief historian of the general staff.

At the time of Schlieffen's appointment, the kaiser was concerned about the threat from potential enemies on either side: Russia with its huge armies and vast territory to the east, and, to the west, France, still smarting from its humiliating defeat in 1871 and jealous of Germany's burgeoning economic and military might. To make matters worse, Russia and France were allies and Germany's only true ally, Austria-Hungary, was weak, a crumbling empire torn by internal divisions. If war came, how could Germany fight two such formidable enemies at once?

Urged on by the kaiser, Schlieffen went back to his history books for inspiration. He immersed himself in the great battles and great generals of the past, studying how victories had been won, battles had unfolded and strategies developed. He became particularly fascinated by the battle of Cannae of 216 BC, when the outnumbered Carthaginians, led by their legendary general Hannibal, had decimated the supposedly invincible Roman legions. Hannibal had swept around the flanks of the Roman forces and then smashed into their positions from the rear, driving them back into themselves. Schlieffen saw that Hannibal's tactics could be adapted for modern warfare, and he began to devote every waking hour to working out how. He studied road networks, rail schedules and maps of terrain, learned patterns of population growth that might swell armies, steeped himself in developments in ammunition and weaponry. Gradually and meticulously, he developed a plan to defeat both of Germany's potential future enemies at once.

In 1905, Schlieffen delivered his Grand Memorandum. It outlined a strategy for advancing on French forces and enveloping them in the manner of Hannibal at Cannae. Germany would thus inflict a quick and overwhelming defeat on France before turning on Russia, which, Schlieffen had calculated, would take at least forty days to mobilise, given the primitive state of its railways and the distances its troops had to cover. A decisive victory over both enemies would be achieved soon after.

PLAN AGAINST PLAN

Of course, Schlieffen was not the only general bent over relief maps and a drawing board in the two decades before World War I. All the major armies were orchestrating their own grand plans for surefire victory when and if war came, as most felt it must.

The French general staff, obsessed with regaining Alsace and Lorraine, lost to Germany in 1871, worked out various strategies. An early one anticipated the Schlieffen Plan and even a possible German thrust into France through Belgium, but it was dropped and its creator, General Victor Michel, cashiered. Having lost in 1870 by fighting on the defensive, France wanted a strategy that emphasised attack and gave priority to winning back Alsace and Lorraine. Eventually, General Joseph Joffre came up with Plan XVII. It called for an increase in the duration of compulsory military service, from two years to three, and then using the enlarged army to drive through Alsace and Lorraine and across the common border, carrying the war into the heart of Germany.

Russia's natural strategy was to use its vast reaches of territory as a form of defence, yielding ground bit by bit but drawing in the opposing army and enveloping it. That was the way it had beaten Napoleon in 1812. But under prodding from its alarmed ally France, General Alexander Samsonov drew up a plan, known as Schedule Nineteen, for an attack on German East Prussia and Austrian Galicia precisely fifteen days after mobilisation of the country's huge army. Eight hundred thousand Russians would swarm across the borders and overwhelm both enemies. Austria-Hungary, facing war against Russia and Serbia (not to mention possible hostilities with Italy, its nominal ally but which it correctly suspected had designs on Austrian territory, and Romania, which also coveted parts of Austria), pinned its hopes on coordinating attacks with Germany, its strongest ally. Germany agreed only reluctantly.

As a mighty sea power, Britain saw no point in fighting a land war on the continent—one admiral suggested it would be 'suicidal idiocy'. The British navy had its own war plans and refused to sit in on joint strategic conferences. The most the navy men would agree to was a seaborne landing and beachhead on Germany's Baltic Sea coast, 150 kilometres from Berlin, as a diversionary tactic; they had even pinpointed a specific sixteen-kilometre strip of sand that would be ideal for landing an expeditionary force. Admiral Sir John Fisher promised that such a strategy, proposed in 1911, would 'keep a million German soldiers busy'. But it was important to Britain that the ports on the French and Belgian side of the English Channel, only thirty-four kilometres from the English coast, not be in the hands of a hostile power. That dictum had guided British strategic thinking since Napoleon. So, in 1911, Sir Henry Wilson, Britain's director of military operations, opened joint talks with French generals Joseph Joffre and Ferdinand Foch on developing a common strategy. Britain, Sir Henry declared, could not continue in splendid isolation if Germany con- trolled part of the Channel coast. The generals accepted the likelihood that Germany might attack France by moving through Belgium. The two staffs decided that in this event Britain's six divisions at home (most of the army was deployed in the colonies) would quickly be brought across the Channel to extend the westernmost part of the French line. In this, the generals were almost reading Schlieffen's mind.

UPDATING HANNIBAL

Ever since 1871, France had been arming itself for a potential follow-up war with Germany. It had constructed a wall of forts and pillboxes along its eastern frontier, so that, in Schlieffen's words, France had become 'one huge fortress'. Its frontier with Belgium, in contrast, was relatively lightly fortified, since Belgium was guaranteed neutrality by international treaty, and it opened onto a wide plain, ideal for manoeuvring the monster army Schlieffen foresaw. 'The heart of France lies between Brussels and Paris', Schlieffen said. The international treaty—'a scrap of paper', the German chancellor was to call it—be damned. Schlieffen also brushed aside the threat from Britain, arguing that if Britain chose to fight, it could muster only a few hundred thousand men. More serious was the threat of a British naval blockade of the Channel ports and Germany; but by the time it could take effect or the troops could be ferried across the Channel, the German blitzkrieg would be over.

In Schlieffen's modern version of Cannae, seven of the eight German armies would swing through Belgium towards France in a giant arc anchored at the Swiss border. A million and a half strong, this force would pound through Belgium to the English Channel, sweeping all French and Belgian resistance before it like a 160-kilometre-long

Count Alfred von Schlieffen

scythe. 'Let the last man on the right brush the Channel with his sleeve', Schlieffen directed in his Grand Memorandum. Once across the French border, the advance guard of the giant army would sweep south, the right wing wheeling west of Paris to encircle the city and attack the French forces on the eastern border from the rear. With the army elimi-nated, they would then march into the besieged French capital. It would be an envelopment in the classic model of Cannae, although initially just a single envelopment. But Schlieffen reasoned that the French might pull troops from the Alsatian frontier in eastern France to support the beleaguered north. If they did that 'favour', as Schlieffen put it, Germans could sweep right around that weakened force and complete the double envelopment.

Taking advantage of Belgium's road network between Brussels and Paris, Schlieffen estimated his mighty army could advance twenty kilometres every day and, on that basis, he calculated where the armies should be day by day. On the fortieth day after they had mobilised at the Belgian border, the Germans would be on the outskirts of Paris, France would be defeated, and German troops would be boarding trains for a high-speed transfer eastwards to bolster the single army posted in East Prussia, along the Russian frontier.

Schlieffen's Grand Memorandum was received by the kaiser with enthusiastic approval. A year later, in 1906, Schlieffen retired, although he continued to tinker with the plan until his death in 1913. Like the other nation's strategies, Schlieffen's plan was kept secret, not only to conceal it from potential enemies, but also from the public and the political leaders and antiwar factions at home. The Schlieffen Plan was known only to the kaiser and his top generals, and not revealed to Parliament or even the war minister. Prime Minister Theobald von Bethmann Hollweg did not learn of it until 1913. By then, it had been in the making for fifteen years and finalised for six.

PUTTING THE PLAN TO WORK

Schlieffen's successor in 1906 as chief of the general staff was the nephew of Germany's great hero of 1871, Helmuth von Moltke. The younger Helmuth von Moltke carried exactly the same name but lacked his uncle's strategic genius or leadership qualities. He inherited the Schlieffen Plan, by now gospel at the Potsdam palace, but with misgivings. He didn't like Schlieffen's overloading the drive's right wing at the expense of the left wing along the French-German frontier, where he was sure the French would counterattack: after all, that was the resource-rich territories of Alsace and Lorraine, which the French had been forced to yield in 1871 and desperately wanted back. So he withdrew troops from the right wing, which Schlieffen expected to provide the massive and irresistible wheeling force that would bring Germany deep into France, in order to bolster the left. But he followed the plan religiously—later students of military tactics would say too religiously.

The German advance of 4 August began with the bombardment of the Belgian fortress at Liège, which put up stiff resistance, not falling until 13 August, only just in time for the Schlieffen Plan to continue on schedule. As events unfolded, Moltke waited at his headquarters far from the battle zone. Due to limited communications, he was unaware of on-the-ground realities and therefore unable to adjust the plan to allow for obstacles such as congested roads, swollen streams that had to be forded, or unexpected resistance put up by Belgium's small army. He anticipated that his army would meet Schlieffen's timetable of twenty kilometres a day, not realising that that kind of pace could not be maintained by weary infantry day after day. Nor had he allowed for the fact that Germany now had many more men under arms than when Schlieffen drew up his timetables; on the narrow roads through Flanders, the troops clogged the roads and halted frequently, throwing the schedule into disarray. Despite these setbacks, however, Moltke's forces carried out the Schlieffen Plan almost to the letter, at least in the initial stages.

Meanwhile, the French rushed armies into the battle zone in Belgium, Lorraine and Alsace, but were forced back by the sheer weight of enemy numbers. Britain was able to transport its entire army across the Channel and extend the French line to the west. The British Expeditionary Force (BEF) comprised the war's most professional soldiers, trained in colonial wars and expert in rapid rifle fire. Their devastating fusilades, which resembled machine-gun fire, held the Germans back at Mons in Belgium on 23 August, but the next day the British and French were forced to begin a large-scale withdrawal.

The Germans continued to push relentlessly west and south, following Schlieffen's plan. But then on 3 September, General Alexander von Kluck, commanding the German First Army, thought he saw a better opportunity. Instead of continuing west past Paris as planned, he turned southeast, aiming to smash the French army. But here, on the banks and tributaries of a stream called the Marne, the Germans encountered something they hadn't expected: a reinforced and immensely determined French army. At the Marne, the Schlieffen Plan would finally fall apart, and Moltke's career with it.

HOW LONG IS SIX WEEKS?

When the war started, both sides believed it would be short. Some said six weeks. Most thought the troops would be home by Christmas. Kaiser Wilhelm even boasted to departing troops, 'You will be home before the leaves fall', and, banking on the success of Schlieffen's plan, prepared to journey to Paris to accept the French surrender. Many of the British volunteers in the August 'rush to the colours' asked their employers to hold their jobs as they would return soon.

Only a few foresaw a long war of attrition. One who did was the British War Minister, Lord Kitchener, who anticipated the need for a large volunteer army for a prolonged conflict. 'A nation like Germany will only give in after it is beaten into the ground', he predicted. 'That will take a very long time. No one living knows how long.'

ENEMIES UNFORESEEN

'The best-laid schemes o' Mice and Men / Gang aft agley', wrote the Scottish poet Robert Burns—the best-laid plans of mice and men often go wrong. France, too, had seen its Plan XVII and doctrine of attack collapse when its infantry was savagely beaten back by the German armies in Alsace and Lorraine. Thereafter, France fought mainly to defend itself and never initiated a major offensive until the latter part of the war. Russia's Schedule Nineteen never really got started. And Austria-Hungary was too preoccupied with punishing Serbia to assist Germany.

Schlieffen's Grand Memorandum did have a huge impact on the war, however, though not in ways its author had intended. It determined where the major battles would be fought—in Flanders and in northern France, and not in Germany. And it ensured that the war would become a world war. For by recklessly traversing Belgium, the German advance made an enemy of Britain, and that led to the involvement of Australia, New Zealand, Canada, India, Africa and, eventually, the United States. Schlieffen had learnt vital lessons from Hannibal, but there was one thing he had overlooked: Hannibal won the battle, but he lost the war.

Russian troops advancing westwards in September 1914

Not only was the Schlieffen Plan predicated on a successful all-out attack on France, but it also relied on Russia taking at least forty days to mobilise its forces. Accordingly, only one of Germany's nine armies was sent to defend the eastern front. But rather than waiting for full mobilisation, Russia sent its standing forces on the offensive as soon as war was declared. Its Third, Fourth, Fifth and Eighth armies moved south to face Austria in Galicia (Russian Poland). The First and Second armies advanced rapidly on East Prussia, where they outnumbered the German defenders four to one. It seemed that the German Great General Staff had made a potentially catastrophic miscalculation.

CHAPTER FOUR

NO LONGER ON SPEAKING TERMS

THE PERSONAL FEUD THAT HALTED RUSSIA'S GREAT OFFENSIVE

One day in 1905, two rising stars of the Russian army met on a train platform in Mukden, Manchuria, with fire in their eyes. Generals Pavel Rennenkampf and Alexander Samsonov had each commanded a division in the recently concluded Russo-Japanese War, which the Russians had humiliatingly lost. Samsonov thought he knew the reason for the loss, and he said so. In a major battle, his division had been under savage attack by the Japanese, and he had called on Rennenkampf for support. The other general had dithered until it was too late, and Samsonov's division had been overwhelmed.

On the platform, Samsonov accosted Rennenkampf, still white-hot with anger. There was a torrent of bitter words. Soon the two uniformed and bemedalled figures were punching and pummelling each other. Others quickly stepped between the men and pulled them apart. But there was no exchange of handshakes, no conciliatory remarks. Both men stalked off, vowing never to speak to the other again. Nine years later, those angry words and vows were to impact on the first eastern-front battle of World War I and have a decisive effect on its outcome and on the course of the war itself.

THE RUSSIANS ARE COMING
Russia's rapid offensive in August 1914 caught the Germans off guard. In the north, Russian commander General Yakov Zhilinsky began an

advance into the East Prussian heartland, planning to drive towards the industrial area of Silesia and the capital, Berlin. He assigned the First Army, led by Rennenkampf, to position itself at the northern end of the Russian-German border, with the Second Army, under Samsonov, posted to the south. Rennenkampf was to strike southeastwards through Prussia's open country, home to the great estates of the Junkers, the Prussian landed aristocracy, the nurturing ground of Germany's military tradition and many of the German Great General Staff themselves, and the ancestral home of Kaiser Wilhelm's Hohenzollern dynasty. Samsonov was to attack west and north to link up with Rennenkampf and thereby form one giant and unconquerable army of six hundred thousand men.

Between the two Russian armies lay a virtually impenetrable patchwork of thick forest, marshes, hills and small lakes. The armies would have to traverse or bypass this maze to link up in the open territory beyond; if they did not join forces in time, they might be attacked separately and defeated. A successful rendezvous depended on timely and unstinting cooperation between the armies and their commanders. After Mukden, that was more of a challenge than it should have been.

PEAS IN A POD

Russia's two rival generals had similar backgrounds. Both were career officers who had graduated a few years apart from the military academy. Both came from aristocratic families at a time when promotion within the military depended less on competence than on birth: top postings were reserved for nobles and aristocrats, with those from middle- or working-class backgrounds limited to company and battalion command.

Rennenkampf, in 1914 a tall, patrician figure with a carefully tended moustache, was of German stock, from the Russian-held territories bordering Germany along the Baltic Sea (which later raised suspicions about his loyalty). He had risen meteorically in the military ranks, being named to the Russian general staff, or *Stavka*, at thirty-six and promoted to major-general at forty-two. He had served in the Boxer uprising in China and was credited with the capture of two key strongholds. Samsonov was a loyal Russian, devoted to the trinity of czar, church and country. He had fought in the Russo-Turkish War of 1878 and served as military governor of Turkestan.

General Alexander Samsonov

A third officer was to play a key role in the impending developments, but on the other side. Lieutenant Colonel Max Hoffmann had been assigned to the German eastern high command just as war broke out. Hoffmann spoke Russian and had Russian contacts, and he knew about the feud between Rennenkampf and Samsonov. He was sure the two would never be willing to cooperate, and he told German high command.

At dawn on 20 August 1914, Rennenkampf sent his army forwards against the German Eighth Army. He did not wait for Samsonov or even try to find out if he was ready—and Samsonov was not. His army had been slow to mobilise because of the great distances involved, just as Schlieffen had predicted, and he was three days behind schedule. Nevertheless, Rennenkampf pushed ahead, and in what became known as the battle of Gumbinnen, tore a hole in the German lines. Then, without notifying Samsonov, he halted just outside Königsberg to consolidate his force and prepare for the possible siege of the city.

Hearing the news of the retreat, the disheartened commander of the German forces, General Max von Prittwitz und Gaffron, telegraphed the general staff headquarters in Germany to announce he was planning to withdraw the entire Eighth Army behind the shelter of the Vistula River. Chief of Staff Moltke was furious, proclaiming, 'This was the result of leaving that fat idiot in command', and promptly fired Prittwitz. To replace him, he called General Paul von Hindenburg, then sixty-six, out of retirement and named as his deputy Erich Ludendorff. The so-called 'H–L' combination immediately left for the Russian front.

Meanwhile, Russian commander Zhilinsky prodded Samsonov to move faster. At first he achieved great success, pushing through the weak centre of the German lines. Zhilinsky insisted that he keep going.

Samsonov protested that German forces were mustering in force on his flank and at his rear. Zhilinsky accused him of cowardice.

Samsonov's fears were well founded, however. The Germans had gained full details of the Russian plan and the disposition of Russian forces, thanks to the discovery of a document found on a dead Russian officer and to intercepted Russian telegraphic communications (the Russians, short of code books in the early days of the war, had simply sent uncoded messages). They had realised that Rennenkampf's forward drive had stopped and that he was a long way from Samsonov. Suspecting that Rennenkampf could or would not come to Samsonov's aid, Hoffmann had urged his superiors to transfer the bulk of the German Eighth Army facing Rennenkampf south, to join an all-out attack on Samsonov. Rennenkampf noticed the movement and even advised the *Stavka* that the enemy in front of him seemed to be disappearing. But he didn't warn Samsonov.

SET UP FOR A DEFEAT

On 26 August, Samsonov surged forwards as ordered. After some spirited progress, he ran into an Eighth Army corps. The armies he had detected on his flank and rear now moved forwards and the trap was sprung. With Rennenkampf two days' march away, Samsonov found his Second Army completely surrounded. He sent frantic telegrams to Zhilinsky appealing for aid or a change of orders, but no response arrived. Whether it was because it was not possible or pride prevented it, he made no attempt to contact his old nemesis, Rennenkampf.

What followed was the most humiliating defeat in Russian history. On the morning of 27 August, the three major corps of the Eighth Army began to close in—two from the north and one from the south. When the Germans captured the key transport hub of Neidenberg, the trap snapped shut. Samsonov's army fought valiantly at first, extending the battle over four days while Samsonov appealed again and again for help. None of the imploring messages were ever answered. The Russians then gave up the fight, many throwing away their weapons and fleeing into the forest. Of the 150,000 men with whom Samsonov had gone into battle, 92,000 were taken prisoners and 50,000 were killed or wounded. The German killed and wounded totalled 20,000.

Samsonov was distraught. 'The emperor trusted me! How can I ever face him again!' he sobbed to his staff officers as they escaped in a staff car. Then, bringing the car to a halt, he dismissed the other officers, walked into a nearby wood, and shot himself with his service revolver.

Rennenkampf was left to continue the battle. The Germans now threw their full weight against him, but he conducted a fighting retreat until he was back in Russian territory. After a second battle in early September, known as the battle of the Masurian Lakes, Russia was forced to withdraw once more from East Prussian territory. He was defeated again at Lodz, in Russian Poland, in November. After that, he was dismissed along with Zhilinsky, and took no further part in the war. In 1918, the Bolshevik government asked him to take command of the Red Army during the civil war. He refused, so they shot him.

Though Hoffmann was the real architect of the German victory, Hindenburg and Ludendorff were hailed as victors, and it remained for Hindenburg to name the battle. He christened it the Battle of the Tannenberg Forest, honouring and redressing a defeat of the Prussian Teutonic Knights by the Slavs in 1410. In the short term, Tannenberg resurrected the German campaign in the east, and demonstrated that a conventional envelopment of an opposing army was still possible. What no army realised was that such a victory would seldom be achieved again.

HINDENBURG'S MEMORIAL

Tannenberg was Germany's first and most famous World War I victory, and successive German governments wanted it remembered that way. Adolf Hitler depicted Tannenberg as the triumph of Teutons over 'barbarian' Slavs, and commissioned a monster memorial in East Prussia (now Poland), modelled on prehistoric Stonehenge with eight vertical slabs. Hindenburg was buried inside it. In 1945, the invading Russians levelled it to the ground. Hindenburg's remains were later reinterred in the Elisabethkirche at Marburg, Germany.

French troops disembark from taxis near the Marne River in September 1914

On 24 August 1914, the French and British armies commenced what would come to be known as 'the Great Retreat', pulling their forces back from France's northern frontiers. Along the way they suffered heavy losses, including eight thousand British killed, lost, or wounded in one day, 26 August, at Le Câteau. Initially, the Allies hoped to halt the Germans along a line running east of the Somme River, but were beaten back continuously. One British unit retreated 393 kilometres in thirteen days. By the first day of September, the Germans were heading directly towards Paris and the Marne River was the only geographical obstacle between them and the great capital. Inside the city's historic fortifications, there was a sense of rising panic.

TAXI! TAXI!

HOW GENERAL GALLIENI SAVED PARIS

'**M**adam, you must leave this taxi!' the Paris gendarme shouted at the female passenger firmly fixed in the rear seat. 'This taxi is needed to save France!' The lady protested volubly. She was en route to visit her daughter outside the war zone, she was hurrying to a train, she would be late, this was unfair. No matter, said the gendarme. She must get out—now! He unceremoniously dumped her luggage on the sidewalk, helped the woman out of the car, then ordered the baffled and protesting driver to proceed posthaste to the Invalides. There was to be no arguing, for this was an emphatic, direct order from the military governor, the forceful General Joseph Simon Gallieni, the newly appointed guardian of Paris.

All over Paris on 6 September 1914, this scene was being replicated. Businessmen en route to appointments, women hurrying to rendezvous with lovers, students homeward bound from lessons—all were forced to yield their cabs and find other ways to their destinations. Under stern police order, taxi drivers were directed to unload passengers, turn about and head for the square known as the Invalides, which soon descended into a chaos of noisy engines, shouted imprecations and noxious fumes. Then, in a steady if somewhat imprecise procession, a line of high-backed taxis, each one now carrying five soldiers and their equipment, tooled north through cheering crowds on a courageous and unorthodox mission to save France. Thus began the 'Miracle of the Marne', a masterstroke that was to win General Gallieni the title of 'Saviour of Paris' and give the French army its first success after a month of losses.

VETERAN OF THE COLONIES

Tall, spare and stern, General Joseph Gallieni—'an imposing example of powerful humanity', as French President Raymond Poincaré called him—had agreed to come out of retirement a few days after the war began to help the country face the imminent threat from the approaching German army. If anyone could save Paris, it was said, it was Gallieni.

Born in 1849 in the French Pyrenees, Gallieni had been destined for a military career from the start: his father, though of Italian descent, was a French army captain. Fresh out of military school, he fought in the Franco-Prussian War of 1870–71, becoming a prisoner of war. Afterwards, he opted for colonial service—what fellow officers jeeringly called *le tourisme*. A dry, precise man who disliked politics, he rose rapidly through the ranks. Having helped put down a rebellion in Indochina, he was assigned to deal with similar rebellions on the island of Madagascar and set up its civil administration. There, he developed the much-admired *tache d'huile* (oil-stain) anti-insurgency strategy, which involved taking military control of a central point, then, through political and social policies, gradually extending influence outwards. Gallieni also put down insurrections in French colonial Africa, and in the French West Indies.

He became known for thinking outside the box. He was one of the first to recommend using aircraft for reconnaissance, even though the conventional wisdom, as expressed by General Ferdinand Foch, was 'L'avion, c'est zero!' ('The aeroplane is nothing!'). Gallieni proved his point in the French army's 1911 manoeuvres, when he landed a balloon and captured a colonel of the supreme command and his entire staff, winning the mock war for his side. By then he was the leading candidate for the position of commander in chief of the French armies. But, pleading illness and advancing age, he stepped aside to give the position to Joseph Joffre, who had once been his second-in-command. After Joffre's installation, Gallieni retired.

When the war began, Gallieni was sixty-five, but his reputation as France's most distinguished colonial soldier was still formidable.

Accordingly, War Minister Adolphe Messimy pleaded with him to leave retirement and defend Paris. Though ill with prostatitis, and grieving from the recent death of his wife, Gallieni felt he could not refuse. After analysing the situation, he gave Messimy the bad news first: the German army advancing on Paris numbered 250,000, the Paris garrison—a raggle-taggle bunch of reserves and untrained recruits—only 150,000, less than a handful of whom were in fighting trim. He would need three army corps for a successful defence.

But he was determined that Paris must not fall. He denounced strategists (including Joffre) who considered Paris 'a mere geographical expression, just like any other town'. Paris was the 'heart and brain' of France, he said. It must be held for both military and moral reasons. Losing Paris would be a devastating blow to France.

TAKING STRONG MEASURES

August is traditionally the tourist month in Paris, when Parisians flee the city and turn it over to visitors. August and early September of 1914 were very different. The streets, museums and shops were empty of sightseers. Few locals were to be seen, either. What were very visible, however, were cattle—entire herds of cattle. In the bright August sun, they were browsing in Paris parks, nibbling on grass and shrubs where sunbathers and lunching office workers normally sprawled, or rambling onto the footpaths where walkers usually strolled. They were lowing and ruminating in squares, too, even in the infields of racetracks.

This was one of Gallieni's first initiatives. He remembered angrily the humiliating six-month-long Prussian siege that strangled Paris in 1870–71, when famished citizens were forced to slaughter horses, dogs, cats and even rats and zoo animals for sustenance. He resolved that nothing so awful would happen to Paris again. He would make sure Parisians could eat.

Gallieni insisted on a free hand. When, at the beginning of September, a nervous French cabinet voted to move the government to Bordeaux, from where they might be more easily evacuated if necessary, Gallieni encouraged them to go (although he later commented waspishly, 'Perhaps one or two ministers should have remained, for appearance's sake'). Then he had a proclamation posted on walls around Paris:

To the Army of Paris and the Population of Paris:
The members of the Government of the Republic have left
Paris in order to give a new impulse to the national defence. I have
received the order to defend Paris against the invader.
This order I shall fulfill to the end.
—GALLIENI

THEY OFFER THEIR FLANK

Gallieni believed that the battle to save Paris must be fought outside
Paris. He rounded up every workman he could locate, and sent them
outside the city walls to dig rifle pits, repair the old fortifications, erect
barricades and clear fields to allow for direct shots at the enemy, turning
Paris into what he called 'an entrenched camp'. He also began to forge
the garrison into a cohesive army, led by his able general, Michel-Joseph
Maunoury, a sixty-six-year-old veteran. And he sent his squadron of
nine rickety aircraft aloft to monitor the Germans' progress.

But it turned out that the Germans weren't planning to attack the
city—at least not immediately. Rather than swing his forces round the city
in a giant arc as dictated by the Schlieffen Plan, the German commander
General Alexander von Kluck had concluded that his more important
mission was to destroy the French army. Cities could wait. So, instead of
continuing his southwards advance, he turned his troops east, to trap the
French forces there and confront the armies from eastern France that
had been hurrying to reinforce the decimated troops outside Paris.

Gallieni had been following the German advance on a huge map
in his headquarters, moving large pins to mark the position of each
German army. On 3 September, the pins showed unmistakably that
the Germans were headed in a straight line east, rather than south.
'They offer us their flank!' exclaimed Gallieni's chief of staff, General
Clergerie. Gallieni immediately saw his chance.

A flank attack on an enemy's rear or flank which is 'in the air'—
that is, not anchored to another army, nor to a topographical feature
like a river or mountain ridge—is every strategist's dream. It allows the
attacking army to strike the enemy from the side or from a wide-open
rear instead of frontally. Gallieni leapt at this opportunity to strike a
decisive blow in what had been until then a dispiriting month for

France. He also saw the need to strike quickly. Nursing their battered and weary armies, the French commander in chief, Joffre, and the commander of the British Expeditionary Force (BEF), Sir John French, had been planning to retreat behind the Seine River and then attempt a counterattack. Gallieni saw that they must drop this plan, and instead attack at once, while the Germans were vulnerable.

In a wild car ride over shell-torn roads, he paid a midnight visit to the BEF headquarters, then insistently phoned Joffre. Initially, the French generalissimo, who mistrusted telephones, refused to answer, but eventually he agreed to talk. He listened to Gallieni's arguments that he must halt his retreat, turn his armies about, support Gallieni's flank and attack and fight in the valley of the Marne River, fifty kilometres north of Paris, rather than behind the Seine. And finally he gave in.

On the morning of 6 September, Gallieni sent his air squadron aloft once again. They found the German flank still exposed. Gallieni sent General Maunoury forwards with his undermanned and pieced-together force, now called the French Sixth Army, to attack. Maunoury was a tenacious and resolute fighter and his swift stroke caught the Germans off guard, just as Gallieni had predicted, driving them backwards. But the enemy force was too large for Maunoury's outnumbered and inexperienced army. His men dug in but were clearly in danger of being overwhelmed. He sent a frantic SOS to Gallieni for more troops.

General Joseph Gallieni, 'saviour of Paris'

Gallieni had stripped the Paris garrison of every last man and had none to send. Then—a godsend!—a train full of troops arrived from the Mediterranean coast. Resplendent in their Zouave uniforms, the Forty-fifth Algerian Division from French North Africa had been heading for eastern France. Military Governor Gallieni countermanded their orders and conscripted them for the fight on the Marne.

But how would they get them to Maunoury and the front, General Clergerie asked. The railways were bereft of rolling stock. Truck transport was scanty. Much of it was disabled and the few available lorries had already been pressed into service.

'Taxis', Gallieni said. 'Send them in taxis.'

STOP THAT CAB!

Taxis? Who had ever heard of sending troops to battle in taxis? It was certainly not in the textbook of military tactics. But then the resourceful Gallieni, who had fought unconventionally in the colonies, had never felt constrained by what he had learnt in the military academy. The troops were desperately needed at the front. Paris streets were full of taxis. They were a ready, quick means of getting the Zouaves to the battlefront. What was the problem? The taxi drivers had already been notified that they were subject to military command.

DRESSING FOR WAR

While other troops dressed themselves in dull, inconspicuous grey, light blue, green, or khaki tones, at the beginning of the war the French army went resolutely into battle in a glorious parade-ground uniform little changed since Napoleon's day. It consisted of a bright blue tunic, red pillbox cap with visor, and flamboyant, ballooning red trousers. No matter that the colours made them an eye-catching target for snipers. When voices—including that of General Gallieni—suggested that wearing something less spectacular might save lives, traditionalists were outraged. 'Les pantalons rouge, c'est la France!' ('Red trousers are France!'), cried a hyper-patriotic former war minister in the National Assembly when the change was proposed in 1913—and soundly defeated. But after the French had seen 350,000 brightly clad men killed or wounded in the first three months of the war, it was quietly decided that a more subdued attire might be a good idea. By the spring of 1915, French soldiers were dressed in a more sombre colour, called 'field blue'.

Gallieni immediately passed the order to the prefect of police and the military's transport division. All taxis were to be stopped, emptied of passengers, sent to their garages for refuelling and then diverted to the Invalides. To the cheers of the crowds packing the streets, the Zouaves marched along the Paris boulevards from the railway station to the Invalides and the cabs began to converge. Gallieni bounced from his headquarters in a nearby girls' school (he had abandoned the traditional military command centre as too big, too fusty and too bogged down in tradition) to supervise the loading. He pushed troops here and there, thrusting five into every cab—three in back, two on jumpseats. Some did not even have rifles. Never mind. They could get equipment at the front.

Should they charge by the trip or 'on the clock', one driver wanted to know. 'On the clock', he was told. 'France will pay you.' Gallieni went from cab to cab, encouraging the drivers. 'Are you scared of gunfire?' he asked one grizzled driver. The old man saluted. '*Mon général*, we will go anywhere we are asked.'

The cabs straggled into line, and Gallieni waved them off. Midway to the front, the strange procession paused to regroup, fix flat tires, cool overheated engines and obtain further orders. Then it headed north again to Maunoury's staging area. The fresh men were quickly thrust into the line. Kluck's army, which had been marching and fighting without let-up for six weeks, began to fall back. Joffre's Third and Fourth Armies and the BEF then followed up on Gallieni's thrust. For four days the fighting continued across the Marne basin, each side parrying for a breakthrough, until the German forces fell back, acknowledging the stalemate and endeavouring to repair their overstretched supply lines. Paris had been saved, almost on its very doorstep.

Joffre, as the overall commander, received credit for the stalwart defensive action. But it was agreed that Gallieni's ingenuity had saved the day, and that the commandeered taxis were the turning point. 'There was only one man who in defiance of all the rules would have ventured an attack so far from his base', Kluck said ruefully after the Armistice. 'Unfortunately for me, that man was Gallieni.'

As a last stroke, Gallieni made sure that the cab drivers were paid. They received twenty-seven per cent of the meter total—the standard rate for three or more passengers, plus luggage.

An artist's impression of the Christmas Truce of 1914, between British and German troops in Flanders

After the battle of the Marne, the Germans fell back to the Aisne River, and both sides dug in for an extended campaign. Trenches soon stretched for five hundred kilometres from the Swiss frontier, along the Aisne and north to the coast. Meanwhile, the war extended to the Pacific Ocean following Japan's declaration of war on Germany. Germany combined with Austria–Hungary to push Russia further back in Galicia, and Turkey joined the Central Powers. In October and November, Belgian Flanders became the focus of attempts by both sides to break through the newly established western front, but a series of engagements, known as the First Battle of Ypres, ended in stalemate. By year's end, more than two hundred thousand German, three hundred thousand French and thirty thousand British soldiers had become casualties.

CHAPTER SIX

'DON'T SHOOT, WE'LL SEND BEER!'

THE EXTRAORDINARY CHRISTMAS TRUCE OF 1914

In the frosty Christmas Eve moonlight of 1914, in the British sector of the Flanders front, Captain Charles Stockwell of the Fifth Welsh Fusiliers peered over a trench parapet and saw a strange sight. The German parapet facing him, some one hundred metres away, was lined with flickering lights 'like the footlights of a theatre'. Then softly across the churned-up mud of no-man's-land floated a chorus of human voices, rising and falling to the Christmas carol 'Stille Nacht' ('Silent Night'), beloved by both sides.

Sometimes, on a quiet night, the men in Stockwell's trenches would hear voices singing in the trenches opposite. The fusiliers occasionally sang, too. But this was different. The Germans were singing in a celebratory fashion, almost like they were in church. Stockwell's mind flashed back to Christmases at home, the joy of being surrounded by family and loved ones. He realised that the Germans were having the same kinds of thoughts.

Haltingly at first, then full-throated, Stockwell's fusiliers responded with 'Joy to the World'. 'Merry Christmas', the Germans shouted in English, adding 'Don't shoot! We'll send beer!' Now Stockwell and his men could see shadowy human forms scrambling over the German parapet. 'Merry Christmas!' the voices shouted again, in unmistakable if accented English. Holding their hands above their heads to show they were unarmed, the Germans, members of the Sixth Westphalian

Regiment, advanced through the crisp night into the now-frozen mud. One even carried a candlelit Christmas tree to the British lines—the footlights Stockwell had seen.

Stockwell and his troops emerged, too. Men who had been trying to kill each other only hours before shook hands, smiled and exchanged wishes for a 'Merry Christmas' and 'Fröhliche Weihnachten'. Stockwell then met the German commander ('Count Something or Other. He seemed a very decent fellow.') and saluted. The two armies swapped candy and cigars. Together, they sang Christmas carols that both sides knew. Then Briton and German retired to the trenches. But the singing went on almost until dawn.

Thus began the so-called 'Christmas Truce', one of the most extraordinary events of any war. Across the western front, and especially in the fifty-kilometre sector of Flanders where the British and Germans had confronted each other for more than three agonising months, and where thousands of their comrades has lost their lives, war took a holiday as both sides set down their arms to celebrate the season of peace and goodwill—together.

LIVE AND LET LIVE

In the early days of the war, the men in the trenches established their own code of behaviour towards the enemy—a code of 'live and let live'. It was an unwritten rule on both sides that you did not fire at the enemy during the dinner hour, nor when they might be having tea; you fired into the air, over the enemy's heads—except when an officer was watching; and you let rescuers carrying a white flag move into no-man's-land to bring in the wounded, and sometimes to bury the dead. Traditionally in Europe, combatants in war treated each other with respect and opposing forces had a sense of fellowship. Some of this endured in the trenches in 1914. The British and Germans especially felt that they had a shared heritage and were therefore sympathetic.

In one area of the British front near Ypres, where the trenches were only sixty metres apart, the two sides had grown so 'pally', as one soldier wrote home, that they regularly tossed newspapers weighted with a stone to each other and sometimes threw cigarettes or a ration tin. They shouted remarks to each other, 'sometimes rude ones', one

DIG, DIG, DIG

A s the war stalemated and troops dug in, no one foresaw that their supposedly 'temporary' entrenchments might become their homes for the next four years, and that they would develop their own lifestyle. Nor that trench life would devolve into an often-boring routine punctuated by episodes of sheer horror and death.

With the horrific autumn rains in 1914, trenches quickly became mudholes, almost canals. Troops waded in muddy water up their thighs. Many suffered from 'trench foot' as a result of wearing mud-soaked boots, or 'trench fever', which was spread by the bite of the ubiquitous body lice. 'The two things infantry feared most', one soldier said, 'were cold rain and lice. Cannon only came third'.

In time, a permanent trench network developed, with supporting trenches for rest areas, supply stations and first aid, and dugouts for additional shelter. Each army developed its own approach to building trenches. The French regarded trenches as way stations, temporary ditches from which they would arise to drive their enemies back across the border, and invested little work in them. To keep their soldiers focused on attack, they didn't even issue entrenching tools. The Germans, on the other hand, regarded trenches as long-term defensive bastions, and often reinforced them with concrete and installed electric lights. Troops improvised their own home improvements. One German soldier wrote home that he had shovelled out a private bunk space and equipped it with a curtain and lamp so he could read at night.

The British had learnt about trenches during the Boer War, where their enemies quickly dug in at the first sound of artillery fire. British trenches were dug according to strict rules and part of each day was spent maintaining trenches. The British were careful to include sheltered areas where they could socialise, write letters and make tea. Even in the mud of Flanders one man wrote his wife: 'It isn't a bad life'.

infantryman said, 'but with less venom than a couple of London cabbies after a mild collision'. Once, a German threw a boot that landed in a British trench. To their surprise, the British found it was not a bomb, but was filled with sausages and chocolate.

Such sentiments became more widespread with the approach of Christmas. To Germans and Britons alike, this was the most festive holiday of the year. It was the Germans who had developed the custom of bringing an evergreen tree indoors and decorating it, and had cultivated the legend of the gift-giving Saint Nicholas, or Santa Claus. Both traditions had been introduced to Britain by Queen Victoria's German-born Prince Consort, Albert.

The British and German governments showered the troops with Christmas goodies—Cadbury chocolates, Callard and Bowser butterscotch, and plum puddings for the BEF Tommies, packed in a 'Princess Mary' tin bearing the image of the king's daughter; a meerschaum pipe from the kaiser for German enlisted men, and Christmas cigars for the officers. The German Crown Prince Wilhelm, commanding the German Fifth Army in the Argonne, ordered the import of 'thousands' of trees plus candles. 'Little Willy', as the kaiser's son was known, also engaged tenor Walter Kirchkoff from the Berlin Imperial Opera to perch on a parapet and sing Christmas songs for the troops on Christmas Eve.

With the beginning of the cold midwinter weather, there was a lull in the fighting, and Britons and Germans went side by side into the fields to collect straw with which to line the soggy trenches. There was so much back-and-forth between the supposed enemies in early December that British General Horace Smith-Dorrien of the BEF's II Corps felt compelled to warn, 'Friendly intercourse with the enemy, unofficial armistices and the exchange of tobacco and other comforts, however tempting and occasionally amusing they may be, are absolutely prohibited'.

Just over a week before Christmas, a group of Germans in an area held by Saxon regiments near Messines, holding their arms up to show they were unarmed, came out into no-man's-land to bring in wounded. Seeing them, the British troops went out, too, and brought in their wounded; then the two sides chatted, exchanged cigarettes, and helped each other bury their dead. 'They seemed extraordinarily fine men', one Tommy wrote home. 'It seemed too ironical for words. The night before, we had been having a terrific battle and the morning after, there we were, they smoking our cigarettes and we smoking theirs.'

A few days afterwards, near Armentières, the Germans somehow managed to smuggle a 'delicious' chocolate cake into the British lines, along with an invitation: 'We propose having a concert tonight as it is our captain's birthday, and cordially invite you to attend—provided as guests you agree to cease all hostilities between 7:30 and 8:30'. The concert began promptly at 7:30 p.m., with the British seated on the parapets, and then both sides joined together to sing 'God Save the King' and the German patriotic song 'Die Wacht am Rhein' ('The Watch on the Rhine').

As Christmas Eve approached, senior commanders became concerned. 'It is thought possible that the enemy may be contemplating an attack during Christmas or New Year. Special vigilance will be maintained during those periods', warned a Christmas Eve message from General Sir John French, the British commander in chief.

But officers further down the chain of command felt otherwise. 'I have ordered my troops that, if at all avoidable, no shot shall be fired from our side either today or on Christmas Eve or the two pursuant Christmas holidays', declared a German lieutenant, Kurt Zehmisch of the 134th Saxons. Another officer summed up the German attitude succinctly: 'A *Tannenbaum* [Christmas tree] is more important than a war'.

THE VISITING TENOR

'No shoot tonight! Sing tonight! Just sing tonight!' one German soldier shouted near midnight across no-man's-land in a sector of Flanders held by the Scots Guards. And sing both sides did, their songs punctuated by harmonica solos, a cornet solo and a violinist who performed Handel's 'Largo'. At midnight a church bell rang from a village close to the lines, and the favourite French carol 'Cantique de Noël' ('Oh, Holy Night'), sung by the renowned French opera singer Victor Granier, rang across the shattered, hushed Belgian landscape. Mixed in with the sacred music were sentimental ballads and bawdy beer-hall songs, even 'It's a Long Way to Tipperary'. 'Like most of my men, I stayed awake the entire night listening to the singing', Lieutenant Zehmisch of the Saxons recalled, 'and it was a wonderful night'.

At dawn on Christmas morning, at Ploegstreet Wood near Ypres, Lieutenant Bill Bairnsfather of the British First Warwickshires (later to become famous for his 'Ole Bill' war cartoons) awoke to find the trenches empty. He could, though, hear the hum of voices. Rousing himself to peer over the parapets, he saw, in no-man's-land, little groups of men in grey and khaki chatting comfortably together, smoking, sipping tea, exchanging cigarettes, showing each other pictures of wives and sweethearts, swapping uniform buttons as souvenirs and even making arrangements to meet again after the war.

Soon, more men emerged, clambered over the barbed wire, and joined them, until hundreds were milling about, even laughing together. 'It looked like a village fair', one French soldier said. A startled rabbit suddenly darted out into the crowd; Germans and Britons alike gave chase and the Germans finally cornered it. One German officer returned to a British officer a Victoria Cross and letters taken from a lieutenant who had fallen dead into a German trench. Some made an effort to demonstrate kinship as well. 'We are Saxons, you are Anglo-Saxons', a German infantryman of the Twenty-Fourth Saxons said. 'We are brothers.'

The chewed-up landscape between the trenches was strewn with the dead of both sides. In one area west of Lille, the ostensible enemies helped each other separate the corpses, and worked together to dig graves in the frozen ground. The British infantrymen produced a pile of wooden crosses. Then a Scottish chaplain, J. Esselmont Adams, gathered both sides together for a solemn service. As best they could, following his lead, they recited the Twenty-third Psalm in English: 'The Lord is my shepherd. I shall not want', they intoned together. The Germans followed with 'Vater Unser, Du bist du Himmel'.

The Germans and British had another shared interest: soccer. 'No troops travel without a football [soccer ball]', General Sir Douglas Haig, later to be commander in chief of the BEF, had said, and, indeed, the troops had brought their love of the game to France with them. A few had even brought balls or improvised them out of wads of cloth, ration tins, or tied-up newspapers. Now, on Christmas morning, at various points along the Flanders front, British and German soldiers started to organise games. It was mostly 'kickabout', without real rules or competition, just men from both sides scrambling after the 'ball', trying to get a foot on it. The terrain was too torn and uneven for proper games, but in a few smoother places Germans and Britons organised teams, and played spiritedly. The Third London Rifles challenged a team of Saxons, chose a referee and actually kept score. The Saxons won, 3–2.

By Christmas afternoon the unofficial armistice had spread across almost the entire British sector. In many places, fraternisation continued into the traditional British Boxing Day holiday, 26 December. But by then, alarmed commanders were making efforts to call a halt to what they saw as a disciplinary breakdown. Although the French had participated less than the British, some of their commanders were outraged. 'If they won't go back [into the trenches], fire over their heads!' one French officer commanded. French artillery actually fired seventy-five-calibre shells into the air near Cappy in Picardy, but to little effect.

British General Smith-Dorrien of II Corps reminded the ranks of his previous order, and threatened, 'On the strictest orders, on no account is intercourse to be allowed between the opposing troops. To finish this war quickly, we must keep up the fighting spirit and do all we can to discourage friendly intercourse. I am calling for particulars as to names of officers and units who took part in this Christmas

British soldiers in festive mood, Christmas 1914

gathering, with a view to disciplinary action.' Some frontline units that had participated in the truce suddenly found themselves relieved by fresh troops who had not yet been 'contaminated' by the air of goodwill.

On both sides, there were also ordinary soldiers who objected to the Christmas armistice. 'This evening I am being told to sing songs with those blighters who killed my friends this afternoon', one British officer said angrily. 'It is a bad show, disrespectful of our dead.'

'Such a thing should not happen in wartime!' a German chided his comrades. 'Have you no sense of German honour left at all?'

THE WAR STARTS AGAIN

Captain Stockwell of the Fifth Welsh Fusiliers arranged with 'Count Something or Other' that hostilities would resume on the morning of 27 December. Promptly at 9 a.m., he stepped from the trench and fired three shots into the air. The opposing officer replied with his own gunfire, and for them and others the war resumed. Their shots had hardly died away when snow began to fall, which then changed into a heavy, driving rain. No-man's-land became a quagmire. Men on both sides were soon too busy trying to keep dry and to bail out the muddy trenches to think about fraternisation.

Yet in places some form of truce continued over the following days, and in a few places went on until New Year. A few days after Christmas, near Messines, a Saxon unit arose in near-mutiny when ordered to fire at the British trenches opposite. 'We can't. They are good fellows', the Saxons said. 'We don't want to hurt them.' 'Shoot or we will', their officer threatened. 'We spent that day and night wasting ammunition, trying to shoot stars down from the sky', one Saxon wrote home. Another unit tossed a note with a rock to the British trenches. 'Be on guard tomorrow', the note read. 'A general is coming. We shall have to fire our weapons. If forced to, we will fire high. But keep down please.'

All through the Christmas Truce, British and German soldiers had been writing home about 'this wonderful day'. Yet it took some time for the story to make it into any newspaper. The French army enforced strict and total censorship. In Britain, editors felt that publication of the story would be seen as unpatriotic; it would impugn the military by implying that soldiers did not wish to fight. It was the *New York Times* that broke the news on New Year's Day, under the headline 'Foes in Trenches Exchange Pies for Wine'. British papers then felt it safe to publish, and soldiers' letters about the 'wonderful day' began to appear in the papers.

However, the Christmas Truce was never to be repeated on such a scale. To discourage further occurrences, the high command ordered artillery bombardments for Christmas Eve and Christmas Day of 1915, thereby ensuring that the men would remain in their trenches. Only a few feeble attempts at a truce were made in December 1915 and December 1916. In January 1916, two British officers were court-martialled for having negotiated an unauthorised Christmas ceasefire to allow both sides to bury their dead. One was acquitted. The other was convicted and received a reprimand—the lowest possible penalty.

Anzac Cove in 1915, showing Anzac encampments and a hospital in the foreground

With the western front bogged down in trench warfare by the end of 1914, the British First Lord of the Admiralty Winston Churchill had a brilliant idea: why not try an end run around Western Europe to strike the Central Powers from behind? Backed by the might of the British navy, Allied troops would launch an attack on the Dardanelles, the narrow waterway that linked the Mediterranean and Black seas and was held by Germany's new ally Turkey. By this time, Britain's colonies and dominions were rallying round the mother country, so it was decided that Commonwealth troops from Australia and New Zealand stationed in Egypt, the Anzacs, would join the main British invasion force.

THE BLOKE WITH
THE DONK

THE ANZACS' UNCONVENTIONAL
AMBULANCE SERVICE

John Simpson Kirkpatrick had 'a way with animals', everyone said.
As a twelve-year-old on holiday, Jack, as he was known to his family
and friends, served as a 'donkey lad' at an amusement park near
his home town of Tyneside, England, carefully leading a donkey and its
child passengers along Herd Sands Beach. In 1915, as a twenty-two-year-
old private in the Australian Imperial Force (AIF), to the amusement of
his comrades, he adopted a possum and took it to Egypt, then donated
it to a Cairo zoo when he was sent to the Dardanelles. In April 1915,
during the fierce Allied assault on the Gallipoli peninsula, this bond with
animals would save hundreds of lives, and gain Simpson lasting fame.

A YOUNG MAN OFF TO SEA
Jack was one of eight children of a Scottish couple and had a difficult
boyhood. His father, captain of a coaling ship, was badly injured when
Jack was twelve, leaving the youth the man of the house. The father died
when Jack was seventeen. He then went to sea to support his family,
serving as a stoker on freighters between Britain and Australia. His second
posting was so unpleasant, however, that he and thirteen other seamen
jumped ship the moment they landed at Perth, Australia. Jack took a
series of jobs, cutting cane and mining coal and gold before returning
to sea again. When his vessel docked in August 1914, he heard the news:
Britain and Germany had gone to war. He immediately joined up.

He enlisted under the name 'John Simpson', to cover up his desertion from the merchant navy, and said he had served a year in a British reserve unit. He was assigned to the Third Field Ambulance Unit and given seven weeks' training for the job of stretcher-bearer. It called for him and three others to carry the wounded from the battlefield to the nearest aid post. His only protection would be a Red Cross armband.

THE FIRST CASUALTIES

The Third Field Ambulance Unit was sent to Egypt for further training. Then on 15 April, 1915, they boarded vessels as part of the landing force at Gallipoli. There, Private John Simpson got his baptism of fire.

The Dardanelles campaign had begun in February with preliminary bombardments and sorties by the Royal Marines. An armada of Allied ships then entered the straits in March, but was held back by Turkish mines and guns. In late March, it was decided that a full-scale landing of troops was the only way to break through. The British Twenty-Ninth Division was to land at Cape Helles while the Anzac forces were to take the beach between Ari Burnu and Gaba Tepe.

Due to a navigational error, the Anzacs landed instead at Ari Burnu, now known as Anzac Cove. The rocky terrain above the beach was covered with thick brush and cut up by ravines and steep cliffs. Troops became separated and disoriented. The Turkish force, commanding the heights, was equipped with mobile artillery which could be quickly moved and trained on forces below. Snipers on the heights also picked off troops as they landed, and dug-in infantry behind the beach riddled the invaders with rifle and machine-gun fire. The sea was pleasantly blue when the troops arrived, but by early afternoon it was crimson with blood.

Simpson with Duffy carrying a wounded soldier

Simpson's unit waded ashore midmorning to find heavy casualties already. Three stretcher-bearers were killed in the landing and fourteen wounded. Four to a team, the remaining stretcher-bearers began trying to reach the wounded in the field and bring them to the beach for transfer to hospital ships offshore. By nightfall, around two thousand Anzacs had been killed or wounded. Simpson was kept busy long after dark.

Next day, the Turks continued to pour down a deadly fire. It was fiercely hot, and the stretcher-bearers slipped and struggled on the dusty and rocky hillsides, all too often dropping their human cargo. It was terrain for sure-footed animals, not young human bipeds. The ambulance crews found themselves not only short of men, but also of stretchers. The hospital crews were simply too busy to return them. The stretcher teams improvised with ground sheets and blankets and eventually began to carry the wounded across their shoulders or in their arms. But it was a solid two-and-a-half-kilometre trip each way from battlefield to beach. Each round trip took an hour, with the men barely able to stop for a rest or mug of tea between trips. 'It was a nightmare', one of Simpson's mates said later, 'even when we had stretchers'.

Private Simpson was well built and healthy and, having been a stoker and miner, accustomed to lifting heavy loads. He worked sixteen hours that second day, more on the third day. In the afternoon of 27 April, on an outbound trip, he spotted a seemingly stray donkey, nibbling on what little vegetation could be found. Simpson went over to the animal and stroked it a few times. Thus, what one of the evacuees, Private Andy Davidson, termed the 'Casualty Carrying Service' was born.

Donkeys had been brought to Gallipoli, with Greek drivers, to ferry water in kerosene cans to men in the front lines. But many drivers had simply abandoned the animals rather than dodge the incessant shellfire. Simpson, the former donkey-lad, saw that the donkey could be a means of transporting the wounded to medical care. He would simply seat the wounded man on the donkey's back, just as he had done with children at Herd Sands Beach ten years before. Then he would lead the donkey and his passenger down to the aid station. He had no saddle, bridle, or halter to make the task easier, but he could improvise. He fashioned a halter out of the first-aid bandages every soldier carried, and wove a lead-rope out of other bandages and cloth.

He would walk alongside the donkey and keep the wounded man propped in place. He decided to call the donkey 'Duffy'.

Over the next three weeks, the man who became known to the rescued as the 'bloke with the donk' shuttled more than three hundred wounded to aid stations or the beach. Whenever he heard a frantic call of 'Stretcher-bearer!' which his alert ear could hear even over the blasts of shellfire and the whine of bullets, Simpson would lead the docile donkey in the direction of the voice, tether him out of harm's way, then scurry through the brush, dodging snipers' bullets and shrapnel towards the wounded man. Then he would pick the man up, hoist him onto his shoulders and dash back through the storm of rifle and machine-gun fire to the donkey. From there, rescuer, donkey and victim would head for the aid station. After unloading their patient, Simpson and Duffy would take a quick refreshment—tea for the bloke, water for the donk—before returning to the battlefield once more.

Soon, Simpson became a one-man, freelance ambulance service, reporting to no one. At daybreak, he would simply set out on his own to find wounded and bring them in. Officially, his superiors frowned upon his actions, but secretly they admired his bravery and left him alone.

Simpson tried to make sure that his partner was well cared for. Seeking better food for Duffy, he connected with the Twenty-First Kohat Indian Mountain Artillery Battalion, which used donkeys to haul cannon and had plentiful fodder. Thereafter he camped with the Indians, who called him 'Bahadur', meaning 'the bravest of the brave'. They let him use their donkeys to give Duffy an occasional breather. Thus the Casualty Carrying Service enlisted donkeys that Simpson named Murphy, Abdul and Queen Elizabeth.

A FATAL RESCUE

After twenty-four days in the stifling heat of Gallipoli, the inevitable happened. Simpson and Duffy were bringing in a soldier who had been wounded in the shoulder. Simpson had lifted the man into the saddle and was steadying him with one hand when a burst of machine-gun fire caught him in the back. He fell to the ground, killed instantly.

The passenger was not harmed. Neither was Duffy, who plodded steadily onwards to deliver the wounded man to the aid station, as he had been trained. Other stretcher-bearers carried Simpson's body to a ditch, out of range of enemy fire. At 7 p.m., they returned and buried him at Hill Spit Hillside Cemetery, at the south end of Anzac Cove.

Simpson's heroics brought recommendations for posthumous decoration from his unit and from Colonel John Monash, commander of the Third Brigade. The ambulance unit asked for the Distinguished Service Order; Monash thought he deserved the Victoria Cross, the British Commonwealth's highest award. The recommendations were repeatedly rejected at higher levels. 'Why honour a stretcher-bearer for simply doing his job?' one officer wrote acidly.

Simpson has since been honoured on stamps and coins and by a bronze statue outside the Australian War Memorial in Canberra, Australia. But no military citation has ever been given. Not so with Simpson's 'donks', however. In 2002, the Royal Society for the Prevention of Cruelty to Animals struck a special medal in their honour. The antique-silver Purple Cross carries the message, 'For all the donkeys used by John Simpson on behalf of humans under continued fire at Gallipoli, 1915'.

EVEN THE HORSES VOLUNTEERED

Simpson's donkeys were not the only four-footed heroes of the war. Although the automobile age had arrived, World War I forces were still very much dependent on horses, particularly as they were better able to manoeuvre in chewed-up terrain. The British army counted one horse for every three men, and Britain's horse owners gave up 165,000 steeds for the cavalry and to pull goods wagons. The Austrians mobilised 650,000, the Germans 750,000 and the Russians more than a million. That did not include 'light-draft' animals—smaller horses and mules—used for lighter loads. By 1918, 475,000 of them were in service in the British sector of the western front. At war's end, eight million horses had been killed on all sides. Two and a half million more were treated in military veterinary hospitals.

British troops blinded by tear gas wait outside a dressing station

In early 1915, it was clear that throwing million-man armies into battle was leading nowhere. So the combatants began to explore other strategies. Germany launched a series of air raids on Britain and U-boat attacks on Allied and neutral shipping, including the notorious sinking of the British liner Lusitania *in May 1915, which killed 128 Americans and brought Germany into diplomatic confrontation with the United States. Britain countered with a naval blockade of German ports. In late May, the Germans broke through Russian lines at Gorlice-Tarnow, while the Allies were bolstered by Italy's declaration of war on Austria-Hungary. But still no breakthrough came in the west. Increasingly, both sides looked to scientists and technology to provide a solution.*

SOMETHING AWFUL IN THE AIR

THE TRAGIC STORY OF THE INVENTORS OF POISON GAS

W alther Hermann Nernst and Fritz Haber were two of Germany's most distinguished scientists, in a golden age of German scientific research. Their peers included such luminaries as Albert Einstein and Max Planck, the father of modern quantum physics. Haber would win the 1918 Nobel Prize for Chemistry for developing a synthetic ammonia, which paved the way for cheap and abundant fertilisers, in turn raising crop yields and reducing world hunger. Nernst, a professor of both chemistry and physics at the University of Göttingen, would receive the 1920 Nobel Prize for Chemistry for identifying the third law of thermodynamics.

But at the start of World War I, the two men turned from basic research to focus on the war effort. They were motivated by a sense that Germany's glittering scientific achievement was threatened by the work of others whom the Germans considered less scientific and less advanced. Nernst was further motivated by the fact that he had two officer sons who had been called up in the general mobilisation and were sure to be placed in harm's way—and needed his support, in whatever form it came.

Ultimately, the work of Nernst and Haber led to the most reviled and feared (although not the most deadly) weapons of war. The type of weapon they devised was to claim the lives of forty-two thousand people on both sides and disable more than a million others in a war that would also bring personal tragedy to both men. That weapon was poison gas.

THE FIRST EXPERIMENTS

The war had scarcely begun when Nernst volunteered—indeed pressed
for acceptance—his ideas of gas warfare. The effects of various gases
on humans had been discussed in German academic circles since the
1870s, and although the use of gas as a weapon had been denounced
by the International Hague Convention of 1899, it had not been
specifically outlawed. Nernst told the munitions office that adding a
well-known irritant powder, dianasidine chlorosulfate, to an artillery
shell would achieve a 'lachrymatory effect' among enemy troops—in
other words, it would disable the enemy by causing soldiers' eyes to
stream—and induce coughing and retching. It was the forerunner of
modern tear gas.

The German Great General Staff at first opposed the use of gas—not
so much for moral reasons as for practical ones. How could one's own
troops be protected once a wayward gas was released into the air and
wafted about by drifting winds? But Nernst persisted and won over a
slender majority. On the eastern front in January 1915, at the battle
of Balimov, the Germans fired howitzer shells stoked with dianasidine
chlorsulfate at the Russian lines. The prevailing wind and overcast sky
seemed ideal for carrying the gas towards the enemy. But in the sub-
freezing temperatures the liquid failed to vaporise. The Russians scarcely
noticed, and the battle went on as if nothing had happened. The military greeted the outcome with the derisive air of 'we told you so'. Gas
harmed no one; its use was senseless. In a much-reported episode,
the young officer son of the later Chief of the General Staff, Erich von
Falkenhayn, won a case of champagne by betting he could stand in a
tear-gas cloud for five minutes without noticeable effect. Nernst couldn't
endure the resulting ridicule. He went back to his Göttingen laboratory
and foreswore military research for the rest of the war.

A CLOUD WITH A LETHAL LINING

Enter Professor Haber. The use of gas itself wasn't at fault, he said;
they had simply chosen the wrong gas. Instead of a rudimentary tear
gas, he recommended a common chemical element, chlorine.
Chlorine was an asphyxiant. Inhaled into the lungs, it would impair
breathing by attacking the tiny, delicate air sacs where the circulating

blood exchanged carbon dioxide for oxygen. Exposed soldiers would choke, cough and vomit. In extreme cases, they would literally drown in their own blood. Chlorine was inexpensive, available and had an unmistakable and easily detectable odour (as every swimming-pool owner has since learnt). That would allow prewarned German soldiers to take protective measures as soon as they smelt the gas. Moreover, chlorine could be easily packaged into artillery shells, allowing it to disable the enemy from a distance.

On 22 April 1915, the German Fifth Army tested Haber's brainchild in the Second Battle of Ypres—with stunning results, if, ultimately, little gain. Facing French and Algerian troops, the Germans were determined to reduce what was known as the Ypres Salient, a sixteen-by-eight-kilometre wedge of territory extending deep into German lines. The German offensive began with the firing of gas-armed shells amid other artillery missiles. Then, in a classic battlefield tactic, the Germans ceased firing to make way for infantry. When the French and Algerians emerged from their trenches to repel the attackers, they were met by a curious grey-green cloud hovering close to the ground and steadily creeping towards them. The first line of troops sniffed the air. Then, as Haber had foretold, they coughed, choked, began to throw up, fell—and panicked. Infantry and artillery combat was something they were used to; but this experience of men by the hundreds falling without being shot was something new, mysterious and frightening. Many collapsed to their knees, gasping for air. Others lay prostrate, yet without a visible wound. The remainder, riven by fear and a feeling of doom, turned tail and ran. And ran. Within minutes, a huge hole, six kilometres wide, had opened in the French-Algerian lines.

This was precisely the kind of breakthrough the Germans had been hoping for since the war began. Now, having created a huge, inviting gap in the enemy ranks, big enough for a whole army, they could send in their cavalry, followed by the infantry, who would envelop the enemy from the rear, smash them in a pincer movement, and inflict a stunning and fatal defeat. The enemy would never recover. Soon the war would be over.

Except ... the Germans were as startled by the sudden opening and opportunity as the fleeing French. German field commanders, accustomed to the ponderously slow advances of trench warfare, were quite unprepared for the rapid melting of resistance and the massive advance now required. The cavalry was situated well behind the lines, and there was no real infantry reserve to throw into the gap. And the battlefield still reeked with this mysterious and alarming smell. Their own troops—indeed, the commanders themselves—hesitated to move forwards and deliver the decisive blow. Finally, sufficient troops were mustered to push forwards and advance the German line a few kilometres, but by then French resistance had stiffened.

Important lessons had been learned, however—on both sides. As gas was used more widely, officers with a smattering of school chemistry recognised the smell of the chlorine. Recalling that chlorine was water-soluble, they taught troops to cover nose and mouth with a moistened handkerchief in the event of a gas attack; if no water was available, they should simply urinate on the cloth. Soon the opposing armies had developed crude and cumbersome protective masks, which the British first used in July 1915 at the battle of the Somme.

A MORE DEADLY COMBINATION

Throughout the remainder of 1915, both sides worked frantically to develop new gases. On the German side, the indefatigable Haber recognised that a gas less volatile than chlorine had to be devised. So he turned his Berlin laboratory into a gas-research institute and eventually came up with an alternative late in the year. The new gas was called phosgene, or carbonyl chloride. Unlike chlorine with its telltale greenish haze, phosgene was almost colorless, caused less choking and coughing, and emitted the innocent, sweet smell of new-mown hay. The result was that it was inhaled more deeply into the lungs, causing greater damage. The effects also lasted much longer. Those who survived the initial exposure sometimes collapsed forty-eight hours later.

To help disperse the gas, the laboratory combined chlorine and phosgene into a mixture called 'White Star' mixture (a white star was painted on the canister as a means of identification), which would spread through the air more readily than phosgene alone. On 31 January 1916, Haber, who unlike Nernst sought to observe his weapons in action, went to the eastern front with a group of officers to witness the first test of the

Fritz Haber, pioneer of chemical warfare

new mixture. It succeeded beyond their wildest dreams. Though only tested on a small scale, its release panicked and demoralised a Russian position, allowing the German attackers to advance three kilometres before being stopped by Russian reinforcements. Exultantly, the German officers turned back to Haber's Berlin home to celebrate.

To her husband's annoyance, Frau Clara Haber was a dedicated pacifist. At his insistence that celebratory night, she glumly joined the chattering group around her dinner table, reluctantly raising her glass to toast their triumph. Then she quietly slipped downstairs to her husband's study, took out his service revolver, and shot herself in the heart. She died in a Berlin hospital next morning. Haber took this casualty in the same stride as others. As his wife lay dying, he left for the front to witness the first use of the White Star gas in a major German offensive.

Gas now became a major weapon in every offensive strike, with neither side having a monopoly on its use. New and more lethal gases were introduced, most notably the fearsome mustard gas. Named for its odour rather than its ingredients and also known as Yperite, mustard gas was first synthesised at the giant German chemical firm of Bayer. It was soon being used on both sides. Mustard gas could penetrate protective clothing as well as lung structure and inflict enormous blisters both internally and externally. It also remained in the ground for weeks afterwards, so that even after the enemy had been driven out, captured trenches remained lethal for weeks.

All told, poison gas accounted for one and a quarter million casualties in all armies, the greatest number—four hundred thousand—being in the Russian army, due primarily to poor or no gas protection. Of these, fewer than one hundred thousand were fatal. However, many of those exposed to poison gas suffered long-term effects,

BEWARE THE SMELL OF GERANIUMS

In 1925, international law prohibited the use of gas in warfare, but not its production. Most countries, including the United States, therefore continued to manufacture and, indeed, refine and stockpile chemical weapons. One of the main gases stockpiled for World War II, along with chlorine, phosgene and mustard, was Lewisite. It was developed in the United States in the 1920s by American chemist Winford Lee Lewis and named for him. Like mustard gas, it is a blistering agent that can penetrate clothing and can also cause severe respiratory damage, potentially leading to death, if inhaled. American troops were trained to recognise its faint aroma, which resembles that of geraniums, but it was never used by either side in combat. Even today, armies and police forces around the world use various forms of tear gas for crowd control.

and gas victims made up a large proportion of the patients in veterans' hospitals after the war, including seventy thousand in the United States. Gas exposure, particularly to mustard gas, caused lasting change in the airways and bronchi in some veterans, resulting in chronic bronchitis and pulmonary disease; those exposed to mustard gas also had higher rates of cancers of the larynx, pharynx and lungs. Mustard gas also caused lasting damage to small blood vessels, especially in the eye, often leading to blindness.

Horrifying and frightening though it was, gas warfare accounted for only three per cent of fatalities, and some claimed that it was in fact the most humane form of warfare because it more often incapacitated combatants than killed them. Others rejected the moral argument against gas when soldiers were being killed and maimed by a range of other weapons. Haber himself said, 'A death is a death'.

A SORRY AFTERMATH
Following his early abandonment of weapons development, Nernst returned to his previous research. He developed an early electric light

bulb, which, however, lost out to one developed in America by a former student of Nernst, Irving Langmuir. He became increasingly bitter about the war, especially after both of his sons were killed. Far from protecting German science, he believed, the war had diminished it. He declared himself a pacifist and gave up weapons research, later devoting himself to hunting and breeding fish. A musician, he also invented an electric piano. He died in 1941 at the age of seventy-seven.

Haber continued to work for the military for the rest of the war. For a time, he concentrated on developing more sophisticated gas masks and other forms of protection against the weapons he had devised, but in 1918 turned his research towards the development of an even more lethal gas. Eventually, he came up with a cyanide derivative, but it was developed too late for use in World War I.

Postwar, he continued his research on nitrogen at the University of Berlin, where he attained an exalted professorial position by the time the Nazis came to power in 1933. But the fact that he was a Jew began to work against him, even though he had converted to Christianity from Judaism to make himself 'more German' and despite the fact that the kaiser had decorated him for his service and given him the honorary rank of captain. Ultimately, for the Nazis, a Jew was a Jew. So what if he had developed weapons for the German military. Haber's weapons didn't bring victory, did they? Obviously he was one of those Jewish traitors who had fattened on others' contributions and backstabbed the German army and brought about its defeat. Despite his protestations of his patriotism, his 'German-ness', his loyalty to the Fatherland, Haber was hounded out of the university in 1934, stripped of his honours and driven into exile. A broken man, he fled with his second wife to Cambridge, England. He died of heart failure in a Swiss hotel on his way to a convalescent home in Italy in 1934, aged sixty-five.

There was also a sad and horrific footnote to Haber's story. Ten years after his death, most of his German Jewish relatives died in concentration camp gas chambers. Their last breaths were of vapours of Zyklon-B—the cyanide derivative Haber had developed towards the end of World War I.

The *Mimi* (foreground) and *Toutou* during trials on the River Thames in England, 1915

Before 1914, the European powers had a tacit understanding that their colonies would not become battlegrounds for, or spoils of, war. The agreement collapsed almost as soon as the first shot was fired, and hostilities spread rapidly throughout Africa, Asia, the Middle East, the Arctic and the Pacific. New Zealand troops occupied the German colony of Samoa as early as 29 August 1914, and in the next month German New Guinea and the Solomon and Bismarck islands fell to Australian forces. In Africa, the Allies quickly seized the German colony of Togo and attacked the colonies of Kamerun, German Southwest Africa and German East Africa, the last of which would offer the greatest challenge.

MIMI AND TOUTOU TAKE LAKE TANGANYIKA

THE NAVAL AFRICA EXPEDITION

In the classic 1951 film *The African Queen*, a prim, spinsterish missionary played by Katharine Hepburn, and a dishevelled, gin-drinking riverboat skipper, Humphrey Bogart, push, lift, repair and sometimes float Bogart's leaky vessel through narrow, leech- and crocodile-infested waterways and seemingly impenetrable jungle to stalk and sink a German gunboat on Lake Tanganyika in German East Africa in the opening days of World War I. Based on a novel by C. S. Forester, the semi-romantic thriller spun a seemingly preposterous tale, the epitome of Hollywood's dictum of the suspension of disbelief. Yet the film was hardly as preposterous as the real-life incident upon which it was based.

AN OUTLANDISH IDEA
Lake Tanganyika is the second-largest lake in Africa and the longest in the world. It extends 1000 kilometres north to south, but is just 80 kilometres wide at its widest point. In 1914, it divided German East Africa (now Tanzania) in the east from the Belgian Congo (the modern-day Democratic Republic of the Congo) in the west and the British colony of Northern Rhodesia (Zambia) in the south. Thus the World War I foes faced each other across the waters of the lake. But Germany controlled the waterway, its major avenue of transportation, by virtue of its two gunboats, and had a third under construction.

In April 1915, a sometime big-game hunter, prospector and Boer War veteran named John R. Lee approached Britain's First Sea Lord, Sir Henry Jackson, with a heroic if outlandish proposal. Why not, he suggested, portage an armed motorboat across Allied colonial territory to Tanganyika, catch the small German 'navy' unawares and take control of the lake? All that would be required would be to ship the boat from London to Cape Town, transport it roughly 2,500 kilometres by rail to Elisabethville (now Lubumbashi) then another 800 kilometres to the lake. Admittedly, that meant the expedition would have to traverse some of the most forbidding unmapped territory on earth, after which the boat would have to be wrestled over a 1,800-metre mountain range and through savanna ruled by the tsetse fly. But given British ingenuity, leadership, and plenty of muscle, it shouldn't be too difficult, said Lee.

AN ASPIRING NAVAL POWER

Even before the war, Germany had aspired to being a great naval power with a fleet that would control the Pacific as well as the Atlantic. Key to accomplishing that dream was the German base at Tsingtao in China, a small enclave that had been leased to Germany for ninety-nine years by the Chinese court in compensation for the murder of two German missionaries. Germany promptly enlarged and fortified the port, establishing Tsingtao as the most far-flung bastion of German military might.

But the Japanese also coveted Tsingtao and, even before entering the war on the Allied side, presented Germany with an ultimatum, ordering the removal of all warships and troops from Chinese and Japanese waters. When the Germans failed to comply, Japan landed 23,000 troops backed by 142 guns and attacked the port, following up with a declaration of war. (Britain, suspicious of Japanese naval motives, sent 1,500 troops as watchdogs.) Heavy bombardments and a protracted siege followed. Although outnumbered eight to one, the Germans held out for two months before surrendering on 7 November 1914, and relinquishing the port three days later. The surrender effectively ended the German dream of a global empire.

It was the kind of eccentric idea that appealed to a British generation brought up on the daring and exploratory adventures of Sir Richard Burton and Henry Stanley, and the First Sea Lord liked it. 'It is the duty and tradition of the Royal Navy to engage the enemy wherever there is water to float a ship', Sir Henry huffed. Next day, the Naval Africa Expedition was born. The navy made only one slight change to Lee's plan. They had recently commandeered two twelve-metre, high-speed motor launches that had been built for the Greek navy. Two boats would clearly be better than one. The Admiralty also felt that a regular navy officer should take command, with Lee as his deputy, since this was to be an official navy expedition. But now the country was at war, most capable officers were at sea. The high command looked around for a candidate and found a volunteer—indeed, the only volunteer.

Deskbound Geoffrey Spicer-Simson had been repeatedly passed over for promotion and had become the oldest lieutenant commander in the navy. It was a well-earned distinction. In his first command, his destroyer had run over and sunk a small boat. More recently, he had been given command of two small gunboats, one of which was torpedoed in broad daylight while anchored in the naval base at Ramsgate; at the time, Spicer-Simson was sipping tea with a lady friend onshore. This resulted in his being assigned to a desk in the lowest levels of the intelligence division. Still, he had once commanded a survey ship on the Gambia River in West Africa. That qualified him, the Admiralty reasoned. Besides, there were no other candidates available.

Spicer-Simson was, to say the least, startling. Tall and muscular, with a short beard, he was tattooed from neck to ankles. Snakes writhed down both arms. On shipboard he wore a long, flowing skirt— a real skirt, not a kilt or robe ('I designed it myself', he said, 'and my wife made it for me'). When he assumed command, he was told to name the two boats. *Cat* and *Dog*, he suggested. The Admiralty demurred, so he changed the names to *Mimi* and *Toutou*. To his crew he explained that these names meant 'meow' and 'bow-wow'.

He had a reputation for tall tales. He said he had shot a rhino in the Gambia River (where no rhinos existed) and a man-eating tiger while posted in China. Some people said he was a born liar. One of his first official acts was to fire Lee, because he was a possible rival.

A LONG HAUL

The first part of the journey, from London to Cape Town by sea and then to Elisabethville by rail was uneventful. Fifty kilometres north of Elisabethville, deep in the Congo, the railway ended. Here, in mid-August 1915, the Naval Africa Expedition gained two traction engines—wood-burning locomotives modified with special wheels—which would pull specially built trailers carrying the launches. They were also joined by three teams of eight oxen, and by 420 African workmen. On the trails outlined on Lee's map, the expedition stretched out for five kilometres.

Alternately browbeating and cajoling in devastating heat, Spicer-Simson drove the group across streams, up hills and through wilderness, all the while wearing his flowing skirt. The push had scarcely begun when one engine plunged off the track and down a hillside. It took two days to wrestle it back onto the track. The first of 150 bridges built for the journey collapsed; a mishap that was to happen many more times. The specially built trailers buckled and fell apart; the trailers meant to carry wood for the engines had to be remade to carry the launches.

At the steep escarpment of the Mitumba Mountains, the engines could inch only a few measly metres up the slope before grinding to a halt. Even the muscles of 420 men plus the roaring engines and twenty-four straining oxen moved them only a few hundred metres. Using a crude block-and-tackle arrangement, the crew tied a pull rope to the engine, looped the rope around a tree uphill, then had the oxen pull downhill until the engine moved upwards. Then they moved to a tree further uphill and finally, two days later, advancing tree by tree, brought the engine and the *Mimi*'s trailer to the crest, then repeated the process with the *Toutou*. On the descent they again had to resort to the block and tackle, lowering the launches gradually until they reached the valley floor.

Soon after, they reached a small tributary of the Congo, where a steamer was to take them downriver to a railhead from where they would travel by rail to the lake. Unfortunately, the river was too low for the steamer, which had anchored eighty kilometres downstream. The expedition had to float the launches and push them, and, like Hepburn and Bogart, have the Africans portage them for hundreds of metres at a time. Finally, they reached the steamer, which they had to share with civilians and their freight, including their sheep and goats.

The Naval Africa Expedition hauling the *Toutou* up the Mitumba Mountains in August 1915

On 22 October, three months and eight hundred kilometres after leaving Elisabethville, they reached the Belgian shore of Tanganyika. The startled Belgian authorities were not at all glad to see them. Told of the expedition's mission, they gave it a one hundred to one chance of success. Unperturbed, Spicer-Simson nonetheless scheduled a welcoming reception and parade, leading it himself in his flowing skirt. Then he set about building a well-hidden port where the *Mimi* and the *Toutou* could be readied for war.

A CHRISTMAS GREETING

The Germans were in fact fully aware of the expedition. A procession of five hundred men, snorting locomotives and ungainly trailers crashing through the bush could hardly fail to draw attention, and word had quickly spread through the jungle grapevine. But they concluded that any vessel that could be transported for such distances could hardly pose much of a threat. They were more concerned about a rumour that the Belgians were rebuilding a steamer that had been damaged years before and outfitting it as a gunboat. For two months, they sniffed and scouted about without discovering either the steamer or Spicer-Simson's small fleet. At one point, the German commander himself made a midnight foray, during which he swam ashore and indeed found the boats. But when he swam back to his vessel with the news, he found he had been given up for lost. He swam back to the Belgian shore and surrendered.

After all the preparation and tribulations, the naval encounter that followed was anticlimactic. On Christmas morning of 1915, almost six months after the expedition had begun, Spicer-Simson was handed a note during the morning church service, reporting that the German gunboat *Kingani*, weighing forty tonnes and armed with a six-pound gun mounted on the foredeck, was headed north on the lake in search of the Allied vessels. Spicer-Simson waited until the service had ended and then calmly ordered all hands into battle gear and to their stations.

The *Kingani* was a slow vessel, capable of only five knots. Spicer-Simson watched until it passed his hideout, then sent the speedier *Mimi* and *Toutou* in pursuit. The *Mimi*, skippered by Spicer-Simson with a cigarette holder jammed in his mouth at a jaunty angle and roaring commands, closed in from port, the *Toutou* from starboard. Their three-pounders were outgunned by the *Kingani*, but the fixed German gun could only fire forwards. When the Germans discovered their pursuers, the captain turned the vessel ninety degrees to port, presenting an inviting target, and increased speed to seven knots. At two thousand metres, the launches were in range and opened fire.

The wind had picked up and all three vessels were tossed about in the choppy waves. Zigzagging to avoid the *Kingani*'s fire, the crews were unable to see if any of their shots had struck home. One or two seemed to have reached their target, but the *Kingani* forged ahead. Suddenly, however, a huge explosion erupted in the foredeck, followed by a ball of fire and a plume of black smoke. The German colours were struck and someone raised a white flag as the vessel struggled, out of control.

Spicer-Simson ordered the *Mimi* alongside. In the heavy seas, it ploughed into the *Kingani*, knocking Spicer-Simson to the deck. Recovering, he leapt aboard and claimed the *Kingani* as a prize. It limped into the British port, as did the *Mimi*, which had been badly damaged. The *Kingani* was refitted with a twelve-pound gun salvaged from a Belgian vessel and added to Spicer-Simson's 'navy'. He rechristened it the *Fifi*.

AT LAST, A FULL COMMANDER

'His Majesty desires to express his appreciation of the wonderful work carried out by his most remote expedition', said the telegram from Buckingham Palace. It also included Spicer-Simson's promotion to full commander—which further inflated his ego. The locals already revered him as a god, in the belief that madness was akin to holiness.

The battle for the lake was not over, however. A month later, on 9 February, the Germans brought out their second gunboat, the much faster *Hedwig von Wissman*, with two six-pounder guns, and sent it up the lake coast towards the British position. Spicer-Simson sent his little flotilla in pursuit, firing as he went. The German ship turned to flee. Outdistancing the slower but heavier-gunned *Fifi*, the speedy *Mimi* caught up and opened fire. When the German captain spotted his pursuers, he turned to retaliate; this allowed the *Fifi* to catch up. Spicer-Simson, however, had used almost all his ammunition. He had only three shells left. The first misfired, and then firing had to be postponed for twenty minutes until it was safe to remove the defective round and toss it overboard. The second shot was more successful. It went crashing through the *Hedwig*'s hull and exploded in the engine room. Belching fire and smoke, the *Hedwig* slid beneath the waves.

A third German warship, the *Graf von Gotzen*, was brought into service in March, but, for unknown reasons, Spicer-Simson chose not to attack it. What he did do, however, was bring his vessels to the south end of the lake, ostensibly to support an Allied ground offensive against the German fort and strongpoint at Bismarckburg. Once there, however, he appeared frightened by the fort's guns. The British commander had assumed Spicer-Simson would destroy a fleet of native boats and canoes to prevent the garrison from escaping in them. Instead, he kept his ships out of range and headed home without firing a shot. By the time he returned to Bismarckburg, the British had captured the fort, and Spicer-Simson was castigated for shirking his duty. That was his last command, and he was soon back at the same desk in the intelligence division, where he remained for the rest of the war.

Still, he had a new repertoire of tall tales to tell, about how he and his little fleet had triumphed over the Germans in East Africa, and of his personal heroism in overcoming all the odds to even get there.

British troops heading into battle at the Somme in 1916

In October 1915, a combined Austrian-German-Bulgarian offensive finally took control of Serbia, despite the arrival, via Salonika in Greece, of an Anglo-French force. The Italians continued to attack the Austrian Tyrol, but were repeatedly beaten back. On the eastern front, Germany conquered most of Poland by the end of 1915, and Russia defeated Turkey in the Caucasus. In the west, the front remained static, despite a continued buildup of arms and men. The colossal battle that began in February 1916 at Verdun, between the French and Germans, would last the rest of the year, cost half a million casualties on each side, and produce no clear result. Rising casualties took an immense toll on armies and on communities at home.

CHAPTER TEN

IT SEEMED LIKE A GOOD IDEA AT THE TIME

THE TRAGEDY OF THE PALS BATTALIONS

To the restive young men of Accrington, an industrial town in Lancashire in the north of England, it seemed like a marvellous adventure. Sign up for the army, the recruitment poster promised, join with your friends, colleagues from work, fellow footballers, church groups, the blokes from the pub, and march off together to win the war. Whole battalions of men who had grown up together, or at least knew each other well, were going to be organised into fighting units under their own local banners.

The idea had first been proposed by General Sir Henry Rawlinson of the Imperial General Staff. Men would be more inclined to enlist if they were going to serve alongside their friends and work colleagues, he said. Lord Kitchener, the colonial war hero and now war minister, endorsed the idea in September 1914. In the same month, Lord Derby of Liverpool, launching a recruitment drive in that port city, helped give the concept a name: 'This should be a battalion of pals, a battalion in which friends from the same office fight shoulder to shoulder for the honor of Britain and the credit of Liverpool'. Thus, the 'Pals Battalions' were born.

WANTED: A MILLION VOLUNTEERS

Unlike the other European powers, Britain entered World War I with no program of conscription and no tradition of universal military training.

87

The country relied on a professional army of fifty thousand men, dismissed by Kaiser Wilhelm as a 'contemptible little handful'. Kitchener, one of the few leaders who foresaw a long war of attrition, realised Britain needed more manpower if it were to sustain a prolonged fight on the continent of Europe. He also recognised that conscription on the continental model was politically impossible in 1914 Britain, which had a strongly pacifist and antimilitaristic tradition, as well as a hands-off attitude towards Europe. Two weeks after war was declared, he sounded a call for one hundred thousand volunteers. By 30 September, more than a million men had signed up. Two-thirds were in locally raised Pals Battalions.

The Accrington Pals were among the first. On 6 September, Mayor John Harwood made an offer to the War Office to raise a full battalion. The recruiting office opened on 15 September. Within three hours, 105 men had enlisted, and they kept coming. By the end of September, the new Accrington Pals Battalion had reached full strength, with 30 officers and 1,036 men in the ranks. Brothers, cousins, friends from around the corner, clerks, carpenters, factory workers—they came not only from the town but from smaller towns and villages nearby. No sooner were the ranks filled than Accrington set out to recruit a second battalion, and filled it just as quickly.

The scene was repeated across Great Britain. 'I would say to every able-bodied young man to offer yourself without delay', a leading clergyman exhorted from the pulpit. 'Go straight to the recruiting office and offer yourself. That is the plain duty of every young man today.' Young women were urged not to keep company with 'shirkers' who declined to volunteer. The men responded. Ulster sent 'Pals'; so did Scotland. Liverpool mobilised three battalions; the industrial city of Sheffield raised the famed Sheffield Rifles and three other units. Witteringham Secondary School in Grimsby mustered one thousand alumni, who became known as 'the Grimsby Chums'. When General Rawlinson called on the City of London, the financial district, for volunteers, 1,900 men quickly stepped forwards and went off to war as 'the Stockbrokers' Brigade'. Over the next year, 643 Pals Battalions were formed, lured by the War Office promise that they would stay together as a unit and serve with their 'pals' from home.

Triumphant with its recruiting success, no one in the War Office—
or in the ranks, or in the home communities—saw the ominous
downside to this serve-together, fight-together logic. They were to
learn about it, tragically, on 1 July 1916.

A GRAND SEND-OFF

As 'Tommies', the Accrington Pals quickly morphed into the Eleventh
Battalion of the East Lancashire Regiment. They were issued uniforms,
a mess kit, knapsack, boots, helmets and rifles, and were indoctrinated
in the basics of drill, discipline and tactics. At first they trained and
drilled near their home communities—Britain was frantically trying to
throw up camps and training facilities for what would become a million-
man army—but in February 1915 the unit received orders to move to a
new training centre at Caernarvon. They went off in high spirits, flags
waving, bands playing, the whole town pelting them with flowers and
farewell kisses. They moved again in May to join three Pals Battalions
of the York and Lancaster regiments, together forming the Thirty-First
Division, a unit made up entirely of Pals. After mock manoeuvres in
Salisbury, the division embarked in December for Egypt to counter a
perceived Turkish threat against the Suez Canal. When that threat evapo-
rated, they were shipped to France in the last week of February 1916.

In a year and a half, the Accrington Pals had still not tasted combat,
and they were becoming anxious. 'Do you think it will be all over before
we get there?' one Pal worriedly asked his mates. After all, the rest of
the BEF had been bloodied in Flanders and at the Marne, and in a long
stretch of stalemated trench warfare. They had learnt to take shelter from
incoming artillery fire, how to conduct night raids, how to deal with
snipers, what to do in a gas attack. The greenhorn Pals had no such
experience to fall back on. They had never been under enemy fire.
Nonetheless, the all-Pal Thirty-First Division was assigned a key role in
what was expected to be the make-or-break battle of the war: the British
smash against the dug-in German line in the valley of the Somme River.

In later years, historians were to describe the first day in the battle
of the Somme as 'the slaughter of the innocents'. The untested
Eleventh East Lancashires—the Accrington Pals—were assigned to lead
the attack on the heavily fortified strongpoint of Serre. The Serre

fortress, perched on a hilltop overlooking both opposing lines, was the pivotal point of the German defensive position. The Eleventh was to head the right wing of the attacking force, with the Sheffield Pals comprising the left wing. Behind them were two supporting units of Pals, including a battalion from the small town of Barnsley, composed of almost all the young men in the town.

Unfortunately, military intelligence had failed to discover that the Germans had been able to dig deep underground shelters in the chalky soil. Officers had assured the troops that the German position would be shattered and the protective barbed wire destroyed by the heavy, week-long Allied bombardment. The assault would be like a walk in the park. Instead, German troops had simply taken shelter in the dugouts, where they were protected from the shelling. When the bombardment ceased, the Germans emerged, manned their trenches behind intact barbed wire and once more staffed the concrete machine-gun emplacements that almost without exception had survived the barrage.

The Accrington Pals had marched eleven kilometres from their encampment to the front lines in the twilight of 30 June, arriving in the trenches in front of Serre at 2:40 a.m. After a long day in the summer heat and burdened with heavy equipment, they were already exhausted. Nevertheless, just a few hours later, at 7:20 a.m., the first wave went over the top into no-man's-land, to prepare for the advance. A few minutes later, a second wave of Pals followed. At 7:30 a.m., a whistle blew. The Pals formed into line and began to trudge through the chewed-up, pockmarked terrain towards the enemy lines. Many of the British treated the assault almost like a picnic. One company commander brought a football, told the troops to kick it ahead, and offered a reward to the first man who scored

A group of Accrington Pals at Caernarvon

a 'goal' by getting the ball across enemy lines. A frisky puppy mascot raced ahead of another unit, with men staggering in pursuit.

Almost at once, they were met by machine-gun fire. Moving uphill over sloping ground, they were an easy target. German defenders recalled afterwards their awe as they watched the steadfast British continue moving ahead as those on their right and left were being cut down 'like swaths of cut corn at harvest time'. It was a form of attack both the Germans and French had abandoned as too costly for little prospect of gain. 'The lines which advanced in such admirable order melted away under fire', Brigadier General H. C. Rees of the Ninety-Fourth Brigade said. 'Yet not a man wavered, broke the ranks or attempted to go back. I have never seen, indeed never could have imagined, such a magnificent display of gallantry, discipline and determination.' Yet, these qualities were of no avail, one official regimental history declared, 'against a barrage ... so consistent and severe that the cones of the explosions gave the impression of a thick belt of poplar trees'.

Soldiers backed up behind the barbed wire were slaughtered. Incredibly, some Accrington Pals managed to wriggle through the wire and fire into and then enter the German trenches. Some of the Sheffield Pals, on their left, also managed to drop into German trenches and fight hand to hand with the German defenders. By then, the third and fourth waves of British infantry were beginning to advance, but they, too, were methodically picked off by the German machine-gunners, even before they had crossed no-man's-land. Most had covered less than one hundred metres.

Without support, the Accrington Pals who had reached the enemy parapet were forced to retreat. Straggling and staggering, supporting their wounded, what was left of the Pals returned to their own lines. By 8 a.m., just thirty minutes after it began, the bloodbath that was the Pals' first combat experience was over. Of the 720 Accrington Pals who had taken part in the assault, only 135 returned unharmed. Five hundred and eighty-five were killed, wounded, or missing. They were joined by nearly sixty thousand others who were casualties on that fateful first day alone. It was the greatest one-day loss and the single most calamitous day in British military history.

The Pals who had volunteered to serve together had died together.

THE SAD NEWS COMES HOME

'Heroic Sons of Lancashire', 'Heavy Casualties in Big Advance',
English newspaper headlines read next day. Soon Accrington and other
communities were to learn the grimmer truth, as messengers on bicycles
brought tragic tidings to family after family. The disaster affected almost
every household. 'I don't think there was a street in town that didn't have
their blinds drawn', one observer said. 'The bell at Christ Church tolled
all the day'. The unit had been decimated, with all its officers dead. 'It
seems impossible,' one survivor wrote home poignantly, 'that all these
people with whom I have lived and worked all these past months are no
more—just washed away. But I look around me, and it is so'.

The scenes of grief spread to town after town, region after region.
In Ulster, it was said, the mere sight of a messenger on a bicycle, who
might be carrying bad tidings, set people to weeping. The town of
Barnsley awoke in early July to realise that virtually the entire population of men between the ages of eighteen and thirty had been wiped
out in a single day. In Grimsby, Witteringham Secondary School was
draped in black; the Grimsby Chums were one of thirty-two units that
had suffered five hundred or more casualties on the first day. Exactly
one year before, eight of them had posed together for a photo: of
those, six were killed in action, and the other two seriously wounded.
Bradford had mustered two battalions of Pals. Acknowledging on 6 July
that a major tragedy had struck the city, the Bradford *Daily Telegraph* began
printing double-page spreads of pictures of the fallen. They were still
publishing them in mid-August.

With these deaths, the concept of the Pals Battalions died, too,
and was never revived. What had seemed a glorious and patriotic idea in
September 1914 was now seen as a horrifying blunder. No one seemed
to have understood the potential impact on a community that had loyally
and resolutely sent all of its sons to war together. Accrington and the
other centres in the English industrial belt felt the effects for years afterwards. These towns were now full of widows and orphans, and young
men hobbling through streets with artificial limbs or wearing jackets with
empty sleeves. Young women who had eagerly waited for loved ones to
come home now found themselves among those who would never marry.
Businesses and factories closed for want of workers. On July 1 each year,

the anniversary of that awful day on the Somme, the town was draped in black in memory of all those who had never returned.

Yet the Accrington Pals unit, the Eleventh East Lancashires, was reconstituted after the Somme, its ranks replenished with new recruits and transfers from other decimated units. It fought through to the end of the war, notably taking action in the important battle of Arras in 1917 and at Ploegstreet Wood as the war was winding to a close. But it wasn't the same. 'We were all pals; we were happy, very happy together', one young Pal sadly wrote home. 'They were such good people. They were fine young men, the cream of the country. That spirit lasted until 1 July 1916. We were all strangers after that. Things were never the same any more.'

THE SHRINKING SOLDIER

When British war minister Lord Kitchener sounded the call for one hundred thousand volunteers, the military had a strict height requirement. Recruits had to stand at least five feet eight inches (172 centimetres) tall in order to serve. Shorter men eager to fight were known to tuck pieces of cardboard inside their shoes and to stretch up as far as they could in order to be accepted. By waiting a year, they could have saved themselves the trouble.

Britain soon exhausted its supply of taller men and lowered the height standard to five foot six (168 centimetres). Gradually, the requirement was lowered even more, first to five feet four inches (164 centimetres) and then to five feet three (160 centimetres) in January 1916. By 1918, half the British Army was under nineteen years of age, and many of them were still growing. Even then, the ranks could not be filled sufficiently to stem the flow of losses, so in April 1918 the Military Service Act was changed so that all males between the ages of seventeen and fifty-one could be called up.

The French army was even more desperate for personnel. As early as 1917, France began to register all boys for the military at age seventeen and inducted them promptly on their eighteenth birthday.

Dead and wounded lie amid the mud and devastation of Passchendaele, 1917

Romania aligned itself with the Allies in August 1916, but was soon overwhelmed by a combined German, Turkish and Bulgarian force. A midyear Russian offensive led by General Brusilov shattered the Austrian army but cost another million Russian casualties. On the western front, the Somme campaign dragged on until mid-November, resulting in 420,000 British casualties. It soon became apparent that the failure of the Somme offensive had delivered a huge blow to British optimism. There was a shift in mood, from hope to despondency, among some British troops and their loved ones at home. Nowhere was this reflected more keenly than in the poetry that many soldiers were writing to give vent to their often torrid and conflicting emotions.

FROM GLORY TO DESPAIR

THE WAR IN POETRY

> In Flanders fields the poppies grow
> Between the crosses, row on row,
> That mark our place; and in the sky
> The larks, still bravely singing, fly
> Scarce heard amid the guns below.

So begins the poignant 'In Flanders Fields', perhaps the most memorable and popular of World War I poems, recited religiously beneath half-staffed flags by schoolchildren (including this book's author) at solemn American Memorial Day and British Remembrance Day ceremonies everywhere. Written by a Canadian Army physician, Dr John McCrae, it is one of an estimated one million poems composed by English-speaking troops as they wrestled with and tried to express their conflicted emotions, frightening experiences, discomforts and longings as the war dragged on and they saw comrades fall beside them.

Expressing oneself in verse was perhaps not a surprising endeavour for university graduates schooled in the rhythms of Shelley and Keats, Shakespeare and Milton, and the drum-beating militancies of Kipling and Tennyson. But the strange and unsettling life—and constant spectre of death—experienced by soldiers brought out the poet in comrades who had never written a line, nor even dreamt of doing so. Just before the battle of the Somme, a lowly private in the Bradford Pals Battalion sat down and wrote this ironic verse:

> We gets our rum and limejuice
> We gets our bully beef
> Half a dozen biscuits that break your bally teeth.
> We gets no eggs for breakfast
> But they send us over shells
> And you dive into your dugout
> And get laughed at by your pals.

After two more grumbling stanzas, he concluded: 'We are here to do our bit'. The Bradford *Daily Telegraph* published the poem in July 1916, on the first day it disclosed the Pals' heavy losses.

'FOREVER ENGLAND'

The flood of poetry began almost as soon as war was declared. At first, it was hyperpatriotic and idealistic, extolling the honour and glory of defending the British Empire and upholding the valour of those who sacrifice their lives for the noble cause. 'Now in thy splendour go before us / Spirit of England, ardent-eyed!' wrote Lawrence Binyon, whose 'For the Fallen' appeared only eight weeks after the declaration of war. Rupert Brooke, the golden boy of 1914 poetry, epitomised prewar romantic idealism and contributed probably its most famous lines:

> If I should die, think this of me
> That there's some corner of a foreign field
> That is forever England.

As it happened, Brooke died of illness in 1915 in the 'foreign field' of Egypt, en route to Gallipoli. Rudyard Kipling (whose tone later changed after his only son was killed) also beat the drums for England.

But as the war went on and on, poems became more sombre, more questioning. Some reflected the soldiers' tangle of emotions in a single poem. 'In Flanders Fields' opens with the lines quoted above, which are followed by another similarly doleful stanza, but then abruptly switches tone in a third stanza that is more of a rallying cry to arms (and which is often omitted in Memorial Day recitations):

> Take up our quarrel with the foe
> To you from failing hands we throw
> The torch; be yours to hold it high
> If ye break faith with us who die
> We shall not sleep, though poppies grow
> In Flanders fields.

McCrae wrote the poem in May 1915, after seventeen days of treating severely injured men. It was 'seventeen days of Hades', he said, climaxed by the death of a former student and medical colleague, Lieutenant Alexis Helmer, for whom McCrae conducted the burial service. He was further moved by the spectacular bloom of poppies around him, and for an ironic reason. Poppies flower only in rooted-up soil, and the battlefields of Flanders, after relentless shelling and burial of bodies, was a carpet of chewed-up earth. Seated in the back of an ambulance, McCrae, who had written only medical-journal articles before, dashed off the poem in twenty minutes, then threw it away. Another officer retrieved it, thought it should be published, and sent it to *Punch*, where it was published in December 1915.

John McCrae never published another poem; he died of pneumonia in January 1918. The poppy became a symbol of the war and is sold during remembrance festivals to raise funds for the care of veterans.

CONFLICTING EMOTIONS

Julian Grenfell was another unlikely poet, but his 'Into Battle' is said to be the most anthologised war poem, capturing in ten simple stanzas the combination of eagerness, anticipation, fear and horror men felt as the moment of combat neared. Grenfell was the son of a nobleman, a warrior through and through, and had spurned a safe posting in the colonial service to fight on the western front. He quickly became known for his bravery and received the Distinguished Service Order for silently stalking snipers and killing them at point-blank range. 'Into Battle' speaks of 'dreary, doubtful, waiting hours before the brazen frenzy starts', but also extols 'the joy of battle that takes him by the throat', referring to the sense of nobility felt by many serving their country. And it describes how 'in the air death moans and sings' and 'night shall fold him with soft wings', capturing the fear felt by soldiers. 'Into Battle' was published in the *Times* newspaper, but Grenfell did not live to read it; on the day of publication, he was struck in the head by shrapnel and died a few days later. He was twenty-seven.

There were few lyrical paeans about the joy of battle after 1916. War was now seen as brutal and unglamorous, and the predominant tone was disillusionment. Poets wrote of the agony of watching beloved comrades die, of grisly, tortured corpses littering the battlefield, of their certainty of their own impending doom. 'I have a rendezvous with death / At some disputed barricade', wrote Alan Seeger, an American Harvard graduate who had studied French and enlisted in the French foreign legion. He continued: 'And I to my pledged word am true / I shall not fail that rendezvous'. Nor did he: on the first day of the battle of the Somme, he was cut to pieces by a hail of machine-gun fire.

Women despaired, too. Vera Brittain had lost her fiancé and two brothers in the war. Of her brother Edward she wrote in 'Perhaps':

> Perhaps the sun will shine again
> And I shall see that still the skies are blue
> And feel once more I do not live in vain
> Although bereft of you.

THE BRIEF LIFE OF WILFRED OWEN

But perhaps the saddest rendezvous was that kept by Wilfred Owen, possibly the most gifted of the war poets. As the church bells were ringing on 11 November 1918 to signal the end of the war, a messenger pedalled to his parents' door with the announcement of their son's death; it had occurred only a week before the Armistice and while Germany's leaders were suing for peace.

When the war began, Owen was teaching at a boys' school in France; in 1915, he decided he had to return home to serve with his friends and classmates. Commissioned a lieutenant, he led an infantry platoon at the Somme and was decorated for holding a dugout that anchored the line for twenty-five hours. He was strafed with machine-gun fire and high-explosive shells at Savy Wood in April 1917. He survived, but with evidence of severe strain, confused memory and tremors. Diagnosed with shell shock, he was sent to Craiglockhart Hospital, near Edinburgh, where he came under the care of Dr. W. H. R. Rivers. It was a transfer that was to forge his reputation.

Rivers was already treating another poet, Siegfried Sassoon. The scion of a wealthy family, Sassoon had gained fame before the war with a series of popular volumes of mostly pastoral verse. By 1917, he had been twice wounded already. He was sent to Craiglockhart partly because he was said to be delusional, but also because he had turned violently against the war. In a far cry from Rupert Brooke, he had composed such lines as 'The rank stench of those bodies haunts me still' and 'Does it matter—losing your legs? For people will always be kind'. He had attacked the British generalship and leadership, writing a letter in which he declared that the war was deliberately prolonged. 'I have seen and endured sufferings of the troops', he wrote, 'and I can no longer be a party to prolong these sufferings for ends which I believe evil and unjust'. He had sent copies to members of Parliament, Haig, and Prime Minister Lloyd George. The government could not afford to have such a prominent poet and member of a leading family

Wilfred Owen with a friend's son in 1917

express such thoughts, so Rivers's daunting task was to nurse Sassoon back to 'sanity' and disabuse him of his pacifism. Later, Sassoon did, at his own request, return to the front, muting his political outcries, but continuing his acrid poetry.

Owen had read Sassoon and sought him out at the hospital, showing him some of his own poetic efforts. Sassoon and his friend Robert Graves, another twice-wounded, much-published 'war poet', at first dismissed Owen as a mere provincial, but Sassoon

THE WAR IN SONG

While some troops were writing or reciting poetry, others were singing songs. In the early stages of the war, most were upbeat. The British went to war to the lilt of 'It's a Long Way to Tipperary', a popular music-hall ditty, and 'Pack up Your Troubles in Your Old Kit Bag'. The Germans had their own 'Auf Wiedersehen'.

Only a few songs reflected the same bitterness as the poetry, possibly because most were written by professional songwriters, not men who had been in the trenches. Generally, they focused instead on loneliness, longing for home and nostalgia—already favourite themes of popular music and the musical stage. Other examples in this genre include 'Keep the Home Fires Burning', 'Till We Meet Again' and 'If You Were the Only Girl in the World', all of which became favourites in Britain and America. One exception was 'Stony Broke in No-man's-land', composed anonymously by the troops themselves, which sharply contrasted military sacrifice with cushy civilian life. The satirical 'Oh, It's a Lovely War' ('Who wants to be a soldier, eh? / Oh, it's a shame to take the pay') was a music-hall ditty that quickly became the soldiers' favourite.

When U.S. troops entered the war in 1917, they sang Irving Berlin's off-to-war rouser 'Over There' ('The Yanks are coming! The Yanks are coming!') and George M. Cohan's hyperpatriotic and bouncy 'You're a Grand Old Flag'. While some troops liked to parody these songs—Irving Berlin's closing lines 'And we won't go home till it's over there / Over there!' were sometimes rendered as 'And we won't go home / We'll be buried over there!'—'Over There' and 'Grand Old Flag', like 'Tipperary', were revived and sung by another generation during World War II.

then took him under his wing. Soon, however, the student was matching or outdoing his teachers, especially in his horrifying images of the war. He depicted the infantrymen as 'bent doubled, like old beggars under their packs' as they 'limped on, blood shod ... drunk with fatigue; deaf even to the hoots of gas shells dropping softly behind'. His talent recognised, he was invited to prepare a selection of his work for publication. Its preface has since become world famous:

> This book is not about heroes. English Poetry is not yet fit to speak
> of them.
> Nor is it about deeds, or lands, nor anything about glory, honour,
> might, majesty, dominion, or power, except War.
> Above all I am not concerned with Poetry.
> My subject is War, and the pity of War.
> The Poetry is in the pity.

In August 1918, Owen was pronounced fit for service and returned to his unit. In September and October, he took part in major offensives in the Allied war-ending advance and was awarded the Military Cross for bravery. His citation read, 'On the Company Commander becoming a casualty, he assumed command and showed fine leadership and resisted heavy counterattack. He personally manipulated a captured enemy position and inflicted considerable losses on the enemy'.

In his last battle, on 4 November, Owen's battalion was assigned to cross a key canal, despite heavy rain and machine-gun fire that inflicted terrible casualties. Owen's troops successfully crossed and held the canal and he was walking among them, congratulating them and encouraging them, when he was hit and killed.

Owen left behind perhaps the most eloquent and quoted poem about the horrors of war and the disillusionment that had set in, 'Dulce et Decorum Est', written at Craiglockhart in October 1917. The title comes from an ode by the Roman poet Horace, widely quoted in the patriotic run-up to the war. After a vivid, wrenching depiction of loading a wounded, dying soldier into a wagon, and hearing his last gurgling throat rattle, the poem concludes:

> My friend, you would not tell with such high zest
> To children ardent for some desperate glory,
> The old Lie: Dulce et decorum est
> Pro patria mori.

For Owen and countless others, after years of bloody and meaningless struggle, Horace's claim that 'It is sweet and appropriate to die for one's country' rang hollow. Now it sounded like an 'old lie'.

German commander Paul Emil von Lettow-Vorbeck (second right) with friends in East Africa, 1915

As the Somme offensive raged on with little result, more isolated and sporadic conflicts continued in colonial outposts. Much of the focus was on the Middle East and Africa. The British had installed a large force in Egypt to block Turkish threats to the Suez Canal in early 1915 and also advanced up the Tigris River into Mesopotamia (now Iraq) to secure oil supplies, but were forced to surrender in April 1916; soon after, T. E. Lawrence instigated an Arab revolt against the Turks. German Southwest Africa fell to the Allies in July 1915 and German troops in Kamerun eventually surrendered in February 1916. But German forces in East Africa continued to offer stiff resistance, to the surprise and frustration of British colonial forces.

CATCH ME IF YOU CAN

GERMANY'S MASTER OF BUSH WARFARE

The South African horsemen of the British imperial forces could not understand it. Their faithful cavalry mounts were standing stock still, eyes glazed, staggering under their loads. Some were sagging to the ground, and looking like they would never rise again. The British Empire had always been able to depend on their hardworking horses to transport supplies and haul cannon. They played a vital role in upholding imperial power. But now, deep in the bush of German East Africa, the horses were letting the Allied cause down.

The South Africans had been in hot pursuit of the German colonial defence force, known as the *Schutztruppe*, and its elusive and intrepid leader, Paul Emil von Lettow-Vorbeck, who had been harassing them since the war began, yet had always managed to escape their traps. On this occasion, in mid-1916, he seemed to be in headlong retreat before their offensive thrusts, but in fact had drawn them into territory where he could make use of a secret weapon.

The South Africans had followed Lettow-Vorbeck's force into the low-lying, densely vegetated savanna inhabited by the tsetse fly, the menacing carrier of the deadly 'sleeping sickness', which afflicted—and eventually killed—men and animals alike. As their trusty animals sickened and staggered, there was no course for the South Africans but to give up their pursuit and surrender the area to the buzzing insects and the *Schutztruppe*. The master of bush warfare had outwitted them again.

KEEPING THE ENEMY OCCUPIED

Such hit-and-run tactics were the stock in trade of Lettow-Vorbeck, the only German World War I general never to be defeated, and he used them skillfully in four years of fighting. The son of a Prussian general and himself a career officer, he had commanded German troops during the Boxer Rebellion in China and helped to put down colonial uprisings in German Southwest Africa (now Namibia), where he was wounded and lost his left eye. In 1914, only a few weeks before the war began, he had been given command of the *Schutztruppe* in German East Africa, considered the jewel of the German overseas empire. When war came, Lettow-Vorbeck realised that the colonial fighting would amount to little more than a sideshow to the main-events war in Europe, and that East Africa would constitute 'a sideshow within a sideshow'.

German East Africa was almost twice the size of France, a land of tropical jungle, bushland, desert, low-altitude savanna and mountains dominated by towering Mount Kilimanjaro. Most of the population lived within 160 kilometres of the Indian Ocean. Colonial settlers had clustered around a few settlements, led by the port of Dar es Salaam, also the capital. Two railways connected the coast and the interior and also led to the colony of British East Africa (now Kenya). The ports and railway lines were vital to both the Germans and the British and most fighting would occur around them. The interior was barely inhabited.

Lettow-Vorbeck's aim, as he saw it, was to keep as many British troops as possible busy, and thus prevent them from joining the fighting in France. Over the following four years, he would more than achieve that goal. Although his force numbered just fifteen thousand or so, he tied down as many as three hundred thousand Allied troops when western front generals were crying out for men.

Britain's nemesis in German East Africa was hardly the stiff, monocle-wearing, unimaginative Prussian of caricature. Athletic, with short-cropped hair and a salt-and-pepper moustache, Lettow-Vorbeck was scholarly and unconventional. He sometimes led his troops while riding a bicycle and often rode the bike to scout enemy lines at night, blackening his face and wearing native garb. He disdained the trad-itional uniform worn by colonial commanders in the tropics—no pith helmets for him—and thought the British officers foolish for campaigning in shorts and open-necked shirts, leaving themselves easy prey for the region's voracious and often deadly insects. And he insisted his European troops live on the local diet of millet and mangoes.

The command he took over was tiny; in August 1914, it numbered about 250 Germans and 2,500 askaris, as native African troops were called, divided into 13 field companies of between 150 and 200 men each. 'Here a company is equivalent to a division elsewhere', Lettow-Vorbeck said. Trained and led by him, two hundred men would prove more than a match for five hundred parade-ground Europeans.

He had scarcely been introduced to the *Schutztruppe* when the British arrived on 2 November. Backed by their formidable navy, the empire mounted an amphibious landing of eight thousand troops, mostly from India but with British officers, at the German East African port of Tanga. Lettow-Vorbeck's mixed force was outnumbered nearly three to one. Contemptuous of native troops, the British expected an easy victory. 'The Indian army will make short work of a lot of niggers', the British commander, A. E. Aitken, declared.

But Lettow-Vorbeck's askaris were highly trained and well disciplined, and extremely loyal. Some were professional soldiers who had served in the German ranks for years. They put up stiff resistance, and Lettow-Vorbeck gave a preview of the kind of warfare the next months would bring. Many of the Indians were seasick after the voyage from the subcontinent, and wilted in the brutal, sticky heat. The askaris fell back into the thick surrounding bush, where the Indians, trained in set-piece, European-style fighting, quickly became disorganised into small groups which were easy prey. After four days of fighting, the Indians were pushed back to the sea, and General Aitken ordered the invasion force withdrawn.

The failed landing had cost the British more than four thousand casualties—killed, wounded, missing and those felled by illness. Only fifteen Germans and fifty-four askaris were killed. And the British left in such haste that they abandoned most of their heavy equipment and armaments on the beach. The undersupplied Lettow-Vorbeck reaped a bonanza of eight machine-guns, 455 badly needed modern rifles and more than a million rounds of ammunition.

A CHANGE OF STRATEGY

Two months later, on 25 January 1915, Lettow-Vorbeck inflicted another stinging defeat on the British, attacking a British-Indian invasion force at the coastal town of Jessin. After two days of fighting, the entire four companies of Indians surrendered. The victory gave a huge boost to the morale of the *Schutztruppe*, and brought another treasure trove of weapons. But the victories were costly for Lettow-Vorbeck. More than half of his best trained officers and noncommissioned officers fell in the two battles, as well as several hundred askaris. The battles of Tanga and Jessin had also cut heavily into his meagre supply of weapons. So Lettow-Vorbeck therefore decided to revamp his strategy. There would be no more costly set-piece battles. Instead he would focus on disrupting enemy communications and supply lines.

During 1915, the Germans were pushed further and further inland, but Lettow-Vorbeck still managed to carry out lightning raids on British depots, railways, telegraph lines, bridges and encampments, including no fewer than forty-eight attacks on the Uganda Railway, which was critical to British East Africa. Cut off from resupply by a British blockade of the coast, always on the move and with scanty communications with he German high command, he developed his own survival strategies.

Forced to live off the land and never able to remain long in one place, he employed an army of native porters to carry captured weapons, ammunition and supplies, as well as barter for food. He made sure his army remained healthy so that it could better cope with the various parasitic diseases that were rampant in the region—the British reckoned they lost thirty-one men to illness for every one lost in battle. Lettow-Vorbeck conscripted members of a medical research centre in the colony and assigned one doctor to every company so that illnesses could be treated in the field. He also had the medics make supplies of the antimalarial drug quinine. When these ran out, Lettow had his men boil the tree bark from which quinine was derived and drink the liquid. The troops called the foul-smelling stuff 'Lettow's schnapps'.

He made good use of his askaris, who were familiar with the terrain and had developed immunity to many diseases, and in return made sure they were treated well. His policy was colorblind: in Lettow-Vorbeck's army, blacks and whites fought side by side, and white troops were often

British navy observing the wrecked *Königsberg*

led by black officers. Short of arms, he liked to attack quickly, then withdraw into the bush, where he could trap any enemy that dared to follow.

Lettow-Vorbeck avoided taking prisoners, as their presence would have encumbered his movements. Instead, he asked those captured to sign a pledge not to continue fighting, then released them. He was adept at making the most of the enemy's mistakes. After the German cruiser *Königsberg* raided British merchant ships and sank a British light cruiser, the British finally trapped her in a shallow estuary in March 1915, running her aground and shelling her until she keeled over. When the British moved off, Lettow-Vorbeck moved in. He stripped the ship of her guns, mounted them on makeshift gun carriages and used them as artillery—the only heavy weapons on either side in the whole East African campaign. He also salvaged wireless equipment and recruited the surviving crew.

NO MORE CAT-AND-MOUSE

By November 1915, the British had had enough of Lettow-Vorbeck and his cat-and-mouse game. Under pressure from the cabinet to produce a victory somewhere, somehow, the British named General Jan Christian Smuts, then fighting with the BEF on the western front, as commander of forces in East Africa. A former South African guerrilla leader who had fought against the British in the Boer War, Smuts was considered an expert on bush warfare. He brought with him forty-five thousand fresh South African troops, making his total strength more than eighty thousand. His strategy, he announced, would be to surround Lettow-Vorbeck and force him into a decisive battle. He developed a grand plan involving a major attack on the German colony early in 1916 by two British columns from the north, Belgian forces from the west and Portuguese from Portuguese East Africa (now Mozambique) in the south. These troops would be backed by aircraft, which would spot the German troops, reveal their positions and machine-gun them. Then the four columns would gradually tighten a noose around the Germans.

It was a plan built on vain hope. Even at low altitude, the pilots could catch no glimpse of the *Schutztruppe*, and the light planes were built of wood and fabric, which soon disintegrated in the harsh climate. On the ground, Lettow-Vorbeck repeatedly outfoxed Smuts, slipping away into the country he knew well, fighting as little as possible before disappearing. The main campaign was called off, but Smuts and his South African forces continued to pursue Lettow-Vorbeck. Soon half the South Africans had been killed, wounded, or incapacitated by disease—and the tsetse fly had claimed almost all their horses and pack animals. Time and again, Smuts would declare that he had encircled Lettow-Vorbeck and call on him to surrender. Each time, Lettow-Vorbeck refused the offer and slipped away.

In August 1916, however, Smuts proclaimed victory. He announced that German resistance had ended and German East Africa was secure. The British now held eighty per cent of the colony's territory and ninety per cent of the railways, ports and roads. King George V sent a message of congratulations. Smuts was recalled to London. Another South African general, Jacob van Deventer, took over in East Africa.

But Lettow-Vorbeck's army was intact, and he continued his campaign for another fourteen months, during which time he scored some of his most telling victories. Van Deventer managed to lure Lettow-Vorbeck into just one set-piece battle. At a village called Mahiwa, on 15 October 1917, 1,500 Schutztruppen confronted 4,700 British and Belgians. The battle was fought with rifles and bayonets on a battleground Lettow-Vorbeck had personally scouted on his bicycle. He and his askaris once more proved their superiority. In a fierce, four-day battle, ground was won and lost up to six times before the Germans finally encircled the British and Belgians, who lost half their force, killed and wounded. Lettow-Vorbeck lost only ninety-five.

But now he was short of supplies, so he moved south and crossed the border into Portuguese East Africa. After defeating a numerically superior Portuguese force, Lettow-Vorbeck's men fell on two rich supply dumps, seizing modern rifles, ammunition, clothing and food. They

A RARE HERO

As Germany's only major undefeated general, Lettow-Vorbeck came home in 1919 to a hero's welcome. He retired from the army the next year, and entered Germany's Parliament, the Reichstag. He resigned when the Nazis came to power and refused Nazi offers to serve as an ambassador for the Hitler regime. After World War II, cut off from his pension, he fell into poverty and was befriended by his old opponent General Jan Christian Smuts of South Africa, and also by the writer Isak (Karen) Dinesen, author of Out of Africa. Smuts, who had always admired and respected Lettow-Vorbeck, arranged for the Allied victors to give him a pension. Lettow-Vorbeck then engineered pensions from the Allies for his surviving askaris. He died in 1964 at the age of ninety-four.

captured 'so much wine and schnapps', Lettow-Vorbeck said, 'that even with the best will in the world it was impossible to consume it all'.

King George again congratulated the British, this time for driving the Germans out of the contested colony. Again, the accolade was premature; Lettow remained on the loose. But his force was dwindling, and even with the plunder of the Portuguese depots, he needed supplies, so he moved back into what had been German East Africa. In January 1918, his askaris defeated the first British all-native unit sent to capture him, and in August 1918 annihilated another Indian force. Meanwhile, he continued attacks on the railways, crossed into the British colony of Rhodesia, and fought his last skirmish with the British on 12 November, a day after the armistice was declared on the western front.

A captured British infantryman told Lettow-Vorbeck the news from France, and the will-o'-the-wisp general wondered what to do. Finally, he decided that it was his duty to follow the example of his superiors. He and his troops—154 Europeans, 1,156 askaris and 1,600 porters laid down their arms on 25 November, two weeks after fighting had stopped in France. Technically, the master of bush warfare had not surrendered. He had only stopped fighting.

A contemporary photomontage of British SE-5s and German Fokker D.VIIs

As infantry and artillery struggled to make headway, a different sort of war developed overhead. The air war began with hot-air balloons, used for observation and to drop bombs, notably in German air raids on London in January 1915. With the introduction of more manoeuvrable models and the increasing skills of pilots, planes took over, initially for observation, but soon also to drop bombs and fire on opposing forces. French pilot Roland Garros became the first to attach a machine-gun to his plane, in March 1915, and the first fighter squadrons emerged later that year. Through 1916, 'dogfights' filled the skies, and a new brand of hero was born.

CHAPTER THIRTEEN

THE ENIGMATIC IRISHMAN

BRITAIN'S RED AIR ACE

Chivalry? Of course it existed! Bitterness and hatred was [*sic*] not
present in the air forces of the countries involved. In its place was
a healthy respect for and interest in the opposing flying men. Ours
was a battle of skill and wits, free of animosity of any kind, a game
more than a war. It was as impersonal as a hard-fought battle on the
gridiron or in the boxing ring. And the Germans and the Austrians
had the same spirit.

So declared the 'White Night of the Air', the Canadian ace Billy
Bishop, whose seventy-two 'kills' of enemy aircraft made him the
British Royal Flying Corps' leading air ace. David Lloyd George,
the British war minister and later prime minister, echoed Bishop:
'The [airmen] recall the legendary days of chivalry. Not merely by the
dashing of their exploits but by the nobility of their spirit'.
That was the image of the gallant World War I aviator: treating
life-or-death aerial combat as a sport played by affable gentlemen, not
unlike 'rugger' at Eton or Sandhurst. The typical British (or German)
airman was well born, well educated, high living, true to all the
precepts of proper behaviour. Such an airman flew to respond to a
challenge, as a knight might have responded to an offer of a joust,
and admired his opponents both for their flying skills and for their
personal qualities. He gave a cheery wave to the man in the other

cockpit, and a respectful salute if the enemy's plane spun out of control or spiralled downwards in a burst of flame. He was the very model of the duelling knight-errant of six centuries earlier.

Then there was Edward 'Mick' Mannock. 'The enigmatic Irishman', one Royal Flying Corps chronicler labelled Mannock, who eventually either became Britain's leading air ace, with seventy-three kills—one more than Bishop—or was in third place with sixty-eight, depending on who was counting. The son of an army noncommissioned officer who had deserted his family, Mannock violated virtually every tenet of the World War I pilot code. First of all, he was Irish—hence the 'Mick' sobriquet. He never attended public schools, worked as a telephone lineman before the war, was past thirty when most of his mates were in their early twenties, was a socialist radical amid mainstream Tories and Liberals, and had absolutely no use, none whatsoever, for the idea of war as some kind of Saturday-afternoon sport. 'I'm here to kill Huns', he said. 'I'm not here to play games.' Besides, he didn't look like a hero. He was short and had matchstick legs. And—unbelievably for a man renowned as a sharpshooter—he was totally blind in one eye.

OUT OF A TURKISH HELLHOLE

When World War I began, Mick Mannock was climbing telephone poles in Turkey. He had taken the job out of a yearning for adventure after working in a similar position in Britain. He certainly found the adventure. When Turkey signed on with Germany and the Central Powers, he was clapped into a 'hellhole' of a jail as an enemy alien. There, he was 'maltreated', to use his term, to the extent that the Turks shipped him back to London, considering him too broken down to be of use to anybody. Yet as soon as Mannock arrived home, he began hounding army recruiters, begging to be accepted into the military.

He got his way in January 1916 and first drew ground duty. Given the rank of sergeant, he was assigned for training in a field-ambulance unit. He found that too tame, and feared he might have to transport enemy wounded, a possibility he utterly abhorred. He applied for the Royal Engineers. Showing signs of the bellicosity that was to mark his career as a pilot, he declared, 'I want to be a tunnelling officer and blow the bastards up. The higher they go and the more pieces come

THE FLYING DUTCHMAN

Books and even comic strips have glorified the heroics of Manfred von Richthofen, the Red Baron. But perhaps the man who did most to advance German wartime aviation was not German but Dutch. Anton Fokker was born in Java, in what was then the Dutch East Indies, now Indonesia. After schooling in Holland, he built his first plane at age twenty in 1910 and taught himself to fly. He opened a small aircraft factory in Holland and in 1914 offered his services to both France and Germany. Only the Germans accepted, already seeing the potential of planes. They set him up in Wiesbaden with a small plant and research facility devoted to aircraft development.

Fokker's first breakthrough was an 'interrupter gear', meant to solve a problem that had plagued aviators on both sides: how to fire a machine-gun through the plane's propeller without hitting the blades. The French flyer Roland Garros had developed a system in which the propeller deflected the bullets. When Garros was shot down behind German lines, the Germans found his plane and asked Fokker to look at the gun. He thought it primitive, but it gave him an idea. Soon he created a more sophisticated version in which the machine-gun was calibrated to fire just after every fourth spin of the propeller. In consultation with the Red Baron himself, Fokker also designed and built a revolutionary warplane that came to dominate the skies. The Fokker triple-winged triplane, the D.VIII, proved faster, more manoeuvrable and stronger than Allied biplanes, and became the preferred plane of Richthofen and his Flying Circus.

After the war, Fokker returned to Holland to build commercial aircraft and later moved to the United States as president of the Fokker Aircraft Company.

down, the happier I shall be'. Still, being a demolitions expert and undermining the German lines wasn't adventure enough either. After training with the Engineers, he asked to be transferred to the Royal Flying Corps. But the Flying Corps rules stated that 'an air pilot must have one hundred per cent eyesight'; as a child, Mannock had progressively lost his eyesight for unknown reasons, and although his vision had eventually returned in the right eye, in the left it had not.

Major Edward 'Mick' Mannock

Mannock, however, had visited recruiting offices often enough that he had been able to memorise the eye chart. But by mid-1916 there was no need: after the calamitous losses on the western front, Britain was desperate for manpower. 'Are your eyes good, Mannock?' the Royal Flying Corps physician asked, when the aspiring pilot returned in August 1916. 'Of course, Sir!' Mannock replied. He was sworn in next day. After ground training, he entered flying school in December 1916 and by early 1917 he was flying in France.

THE SHORT LIFE OF A PILOT

The Royal Flying Corps (like its German, French and Austrian counterparts) was taking heavy casualties in 1917. According to one calculation, the average life expectancy of a British scout pilot was three weeks; a combat pilot was considered seasoned if he lasted six months. Not only enemy (and sometimes friendly) fire was responsible. The planes themselves were fragile contrivances, made of thin wood and fabric, barely held together with wire. There were as many crash landings as safe ones—on his first flight in France, Mannock lost half of the bottom wing of his biplane, although he managed to crash-land it. Flying above three thousand metres without an oxygen supply and then descending to the ground gave many flyers the 'bends' because of the change in atmospheric pressure. The mental strain of flying (usually) four missions a day at dawn and dusk, constantly facing death, took a heavy toll, too. Mannock suffered at least two attacks of nerves, and even Germany's fabled Red Baron, Manfred von Richthofen, grounded himself once for the same reason.

At first, fellow flyers questioned Mannock's courage. In his first two months as a combat pilot, the man who was later to claim seventy-three kills shot down only one enemy aircraft. 'They didn't actually call him "yellow"', his commanding officer, Captain G. L. Lloyd said of the fledgling flyer, 'but many secret murmurings of an unsavoury nature reached my ears. He was accused of being continually in the air practising aerial gunnery as a pretence. The innuendo was that he was suffering from cold feet'. Lloyd called him in, and Mannock admitted to being frightened, 'against my will'. But, he told Lloyd, 'I have now conquered this defect, and having conquered myself, I can conquer the Hun'. With no one to replace him, Lloyd sent 'the enigmatic Irishman' back aloft. Mannock quickly transformed himself into a ruthless killing machine, notorious for emptying his ammunition at an enemy even when the German was going down in flames and the pilot had no chance of survival.

One of Mannock's fellow pilots, the South African Van Ira, described the Mannock method, not without some queasiness, on a day when 'the master', as Ira called him, downed four German scout planes and a two-seater with a combination of deft manoeuvring and skilled gunnery:

One he shot to pieces after firing a long burst from directly behind and above; another he crashed—it spun into the ground after being hit by a deflection shot; the other, a silver bird, he had a fine set-to with, while his patrol watched the master at work. First they waltzed around like a couple of turkey cocks, Mick being right on his adversary's tail. Then the Pfalz [the German plane] half-rolled and fell a few hundred feet [one hundred metres] beneath him. Mick followed, firing as soon as he got into position. The Hun then looped—Mick looped too, coming out behind and above his opponent and firing short bursts. The Pfalz then spun—Mick spun also, firing as he spun. The Hun eventually pulled out; Mick was fast on his tail. They were now down to four thousand feet [twelve hundred metres]. The Pfalz now started twisting and turning, a sure sign of 'wind-up' [that he was abandoning the duel]. After a short burst close up, Mick administered the coup de grâce. The poor fellow went down headlong and crashed.

This was a really remarkable exhibition of cruel, cool, calculating Hun-strafing. A marvellous show. I felt sorry for the poor Hun. He put up a wonderful show of defensive fighting.

MANNOCK THE TEACHER

By the late summer of 1917, the once-reluctant Mannock had scored twenty kills. He had been promoted to captain (and later to major) and named flight leader with responsibility for training new pilots, a job he took seriously; like Germany's Red Baron, von Richthofen, he insisted on accompanying a newcomer aloft on his first mission, schooling him in his work. He proved an excellent teacher, imparting his own methods of manoeuvre and bluff, and especially the importance of marksmanship. 'Sight your own guns', he would say. 'The armourer doesn't fire them in combat. You do.'

Mannock was unyielding in his deep hatred for the Germans. When Richthofen was shot down by ground fire and crashed and died behind British lines, the Royal Flying Corps pilots held an elaborate funeral in tribute to their 'worthy foe'. Mannock walked out in disgust. 'I hope the bastard roasted all the way down', he said. He took to flying out alone, early, so he could stay high, hopefully concealed by clouds, and then dive down, guns blazing, on an unsuspecting enemy. He even took to lurking near German airfields, waiting for planes to take off and give him an easy kill.

Mannock often boasted about these victories, a trait that didn't sit well with other pilots who still considered aerial warfare a gentlemanly sport. He referred to 'Huns' shot down afire as 'flamerinos'. One day he shot down four of them, then on his return rushed into the mess shouting. 'Flamerino, flamerino, flamerino! Sizzle, sizzle, sizzle, wonk!', using his hands in the classic airman style to depict the downward arc of his unfortunate victims. Some of those who regarded Mannock as ungentlemanly and unsporting were sceptical about his rapidly rising tally. Pilots reported their own kills after returning home, then flight officers sought out witnesses—other pilots or ground crews—to confirm the kill. Mannock ultimately reported seventy-three kills but only sixty-eight were confirmed by others.

But Mannock had his playful side, too. He organised a 'bombing raid' on a rival squadron, dropping oranges as bombs; the other squadron retaliated next day with bananas. A dedicated socialist, he provoked political arguments and once organised a mock Parliament. 'We had two things in common', another flyer said of him. 'We were both Irish, and we both loved a good argument. He usually won the argument, but heaven knows what his views really were.'

Mannock's playfulness alternated with black moods. If a fellow flyer was shot down, he often burst out crying. When his close friend and early mentor, the ace James McCudden, died in a crash, he was incapacitated for nearly a week. He became obsessed with death, and was convinced he would not survive the war. When he scored his seventy-second kill, tying him with Bishop, another flyer congratulated him: 'They'll be rolling out the red carpet for you after the war, Mick'. Mannock shook his head. 'There won't be any "after the war" for me', he said.

FEAR OF FIRE

Like many across the world, Mannock contracted influenza in 1918, in his case apparently during a home leave. He returned to duty weak and apologising for his weakness. The sturdy hands that had made him a sure shot were now trembling. But as a major and squadron leader, he felt he had to carry on.

On the morning of 22 July 1918, the still-achy Mannock went aloft with a new pilot, Donald Inglis. The two planes hovered around twelve hundred metres, then Mannock spotted an enemy plane. Waggling his wings to signal Inglis to follow him, Mannock zoomed down on the German, guns ripping into the aircraft. As flames enveloped the enemy pilot, Mannock continued to fire, pursuing his quarry close to the ground, violating an unofficial rule that low flying should be avoided because of the danger of rifle fire. Inglis, following, realised they were too close to the ground. 'I saw a flame come out of the side of Mick's machine', he recalled afterwards. 'It grew bigger and bigger. Mick's nose dropped slightly and he went into a slow right-hand turn about twice, and then hit the ground in a burst of flame.'

That morning Mannock had scored his seventy-third kill. Or possibly his sixty-eighth. Doubt still surrounded his record. Thus, it was not until 1922 that he was posthumously awarded Britain's highest decoration, the Victoria Cross. Which had already gone to several men whom Mannock had trained.

The British Grand Fleet off Scapa Flow, Scotland, in 1916

Expected British dominance of the naval war was threatened early on by German U-boats and by rogue German cruisers prowling far-flung waters, most notably a wide-ranging squadron commanded by Admiral Maximilian von Spee. On 1 November 1914, the Royal Navy suffered its worst defeat in a hundred years, when Spee's force destroyed the HMS Monmouth *and HMS* Good Hope, *with the loss of all 1,600 crew, at Coronel, Chile. After the British sank five of Spee's ships at Port Stanley in the Falkland Islands on 8 December 1914, however, Allied control of the high seas was firmer and became stronger still with the steady expansion of the British fleet and a German agreement in May 1916 to halt U-boat attacks on merchant shipping. But, occasionally, the Germans struck back.*

THE SEA DEVIL

HOW ONE GERMAN SAILOR WREAKED HAVOC ON ALLIED SHIPPING

Count Felix von Luckner had a naval career that was unorthodox, to say the least. He commanded a three-masted sailing vessel in the age of steam and the battleship. He was accused of sea piracy long after the days of Drake and the hanging of Captain Kidd. And his remarkable World War I triumphs were scored in the Southern Hemisphere, far from the major naval arenas of the North Sea, the Mediterranean and the North Atlantic.

In nine months in 1917, his windjammer, the *Seeadler* (*Sea Eagle*), managed to sink sixteen merchant vessels, confiscate approximately thirty-five million dollars worth of cargo, take more than three hundred prisoners, and wreak havoc on Allied shipping in both the Atlantic and Pacific oceans. Yet no captives walked the *Sea Eagle*'s plank; indeed, Luckner proudly boasted that he never killed anyone. The only casualty of his raids was a luckless seaman scalded to death when a stray shell broke a steampipe (for which Luckner apologised to the enemy's captain and expressed his sympathy).

Though his ship was the *Sea Eagle*, to his outfoxed opponents this wily campaigner soon became known by another name: the Sea Devil.

THE CAVALRYMAN GOES TO SEA

The son of a Prussian nobleman, Felix von Luckner seemed destined from birth for a career in the cavalry, just like his great-grandfather,

grandfather and father before him. Felix's great-grandfather had founded his own mercenary cavalry regiment, the Luckner Hussars, which fought for pay under most European flags and served both the French king and the revolutionaries during the French Revolution; he wound up a Marshal of France and was then dispatched by guillotine during the Reign of Terror. Felix's father had tried to enlist again, at the age of ninety, when World War I broke out, and protested vehemently when he was rejected.

AT LAST, THE BATTLESHIPS

Britain's admirals had always scorned the land war and declared that the war would eventually be decided on the high seas. They envisioned a decisive Trafalgar-like battle of mammoth dreadnoughts blasting broadsides at enemies barely glimpsed on the horizon. Both the Germans and British had been frantically building and preparing for this ultimate day. But after the war started, the German High Seas Fleet remained in its port at Kiel. Then on 31 May 1916, an aggressive new commander, Reinhard Schneer, decided to dare the British by venturing out to bombard British Channel ports, backed up by the rest of the fleet. But the British had broken the German code and knew his plans. They sent out a fast cruiser fleet to intercept him, followed by the heavy guns of sixteen mammoth battleships. The British cruisers shelled the Germans, causing heavy damage, then turned back to draw the Germans into contact with the full British Grand Fleet off the coast of Denmark.

Over the next two days, dozens of ships fought in the battle of Jutland, the greatest naval battle since Trafalgar, before the Germans turned tail for home. The British suffered greater losses—three battlecruisers, four armoured cruisers and eight destroyers went to the bottom compared with Germany's losses of two battleships, four light cruisers and five destroyers. The British dead numbered 6,094, the German 2,551. Nevertheless the British claimed victory, since the High Seas Fleet returned to port, never to emerge again. A German journalist described the battle as 'an assault on the jailer, followed by a return to jail'.

When the young Felix began to play with boats, his father discarded them and said, 'You will be a cavalryman, my son', and sent him off to school. After being caned for misbehaviour and failing an examination, the well-built, husky thirteen-year-old ran away to sea, like many other restive young people of his time. He signed on as a cabin boy on a Hamburg freighter bound for Australia and didn't return to Germany for seven years—long enough for his family to give him up for dead.

Those seven years were a whirlwind of sea passages, jobs and outlandish experiences. He jumped ship in Australia and, between stints as a seaman, worked as a kangaroo hunter, prizefighter, wrestler, beachcomber, assistant lighthouse-keeper (which job he fled when he was caught dallying with the lighthouse-keeper's daughter), fisherman and bartender. He joined the Mexican army and was a palace guard for Mexico's dictator-president Porfirio Díaz. He served a jail term in Chile for allegedly stealing pigs. In 1906, aged twenty, he entered a German navigation school and earned his mate's licence. He then served nine months on a passenger liner operating between Hamburg and South America, and parlayed that experience into a year's navy service so that he would qualify for a commission. In 1912, the young officer was assigned to the battleship *Kronprinz Wilhelm*, on which he commanded a gun turret during the 1916 battle of Jutland.

Early in the war, Germany converted a fleet of passenger ships and freighters into armed raiders, equipping them with guns and sending them to prey on Allied merchant shipping. By mid-1915, the raiders had all been sunk or impounded. But in late 1916, the idea was revived. One of the first raiders to be commissioned thereafter was an impounded 1,425-tonne, three-masted sailing ship called the *Pass of Balmaha*. The navy equipped the *Pass of Balmaha* with two 8.8-centimetre guns hidden behind removable gunwales, machine-guns and twin five-hundred-horsepower auxiliary engines, and changed its name to the *Sea Eagle*. Luckner was named commander, largely because he was one of the few naval officers in the steam-powered navy with experience of sailing ships.

FEIGNING NEUTRALITY

Four days before Christmas 1916, the *Sea Eagle* set out from Hamburg. It slipped through the British blockade during a heavy storm and entered the North Sea. At its stern waved the red-white-and-blue flag of neutral Norway, and its ship's papers showed that it was the Norwegian ship *Irma*. Luckner had carefully selected his crew of six officers and thirty-seven men for their ability to speak passable Norwegian. They held dress rehearsals on how to react and what to say in Norwegian if they were stopped, and even dressed one of the men in women's clothes to pose as the captain's wife—Norwegian skippers often brought their wives along on voyages, Luckner said.

On Christmas Day, the ship's disguise was put to the test. Off Greenland, it was halted by a British armed merchant cruiser, boarded, subjected to search and a review of the ship's papers, which Luckner had smeared and defaced to make them illegible, supposedly as a result of a storm. Luckner invited the cruiser captain to his cabin for a Christmas drink and the *Irma/Sea Eagle* passed the inspection successfully.

The ship then headed south down the coast of Africa. On 9 January, Luckner spied his first victim, a single-funnelled steamer, the 3,418-tonne *Gladys Royal*, which was carrying coal from Cardiff, Wales, to Buenos Aires in Argentina. Luckner ran up a flag asking for a time signal, not an uncommon move for a sailing vessel without wireless and long out of contact with land. When the *Sea Eagle* got close enough that the *Gladys Royal* could not escape, it raised the German ensign. Three shots from the *Sea Eagle*'s guns brought the *Gladys Royal* to a halt. Luckner's crew boarded, stripped the ship of provisions and useable supplies, took the crew prisoner, and then planted a time bomb in the hold. Sailing away, Luckner heard and saw the ship blow up and sink.

Next day, the *Sea Eagle* encountered another vessel that at first refused to identify itself. It turned out to be the British *Lundy Island*, which was carrying sugar—a wartime rarity—from Madagascar. When the ship disobeyed Luckner's order to stop, he fired four shots to bring it to a halt. The ship stopped and lowered its boats. Luckner's men boarded; but by then the crew had abandoned ship, leaving only the captain aboard. He explained that he had failed to stop because he had been stopped previously and signed an agreement not to engage in any more wartime activity. Since he had violated this parole, he feared he might now be hanged. Luckner invited him aboard, gave him a cabin, stripped the *Lundy Island* of anything worthwhile, and scuttled it with shellfire.

Felix von Luckner, the great survivor, in 1960

Thus, Luckner's pattern of attack was established: approach a ship while pretending to be Dutch, Norwegian or Danish, run up the German flag once close, fire a warning shot to halt the vessel, board it, seize the cargo, make prisoners of the crew and scuttle the boat with a bomb or gunfire. Throughout his escapades he avoided raiding vessels that seemed to have wireless capabilities, lest the British navy learn of his raids and his whereabouts; for the same reason, he did not release prisoners because they might spread the alarm.

After he had sunk the *Gladys Royal* and *Lundy Island*, Luckner had fifty-six prisoners, or 'guests' as he called them. Under the rules of war, he could not put them to work, but he thought of another way to employ them. He offered ten pounds sterling and a bottle of champagne to the first man who could spot a potential target vessel. 'You never saw men go up the rigging so fast', he said after the announcement. Once, when three 'lookouts' claimed to have seen a vessel at the same time, he had to make triplicate awards. That night 'the champagne flowed freely and our decks became a veritable beer garden', he wrote.

With his lookouts' help, Luckner quickly added to his roster of victims. On 21 January, he met the three-masted *Charles Gounod*, carrying corn to Bordeaux. 'What news of the war?' the ship signalled, and displayed the French tricolor. Luckner approached, then ran up the German ensign. He gave the captain what news he had of German victories, then took prisoners and regretfully sank the vessel. 'I always hated to scuttle a sailing ship', he said. 'Steamers were another matter.'

Next came the schooner *Perce*, which he sank after taking off the captain and his new bride; the French *Antonin*, carrying saltpetre from Chile, critical in munitions manufacture; the Italian *Buenos Ayres*, also carrying saltpetre; and the British *Pinmore*, carrying grain. Luckner had served on the *Pinmore* in his freewheeling seafaring days. He took it into Rio de Janeiro to get more supplies and then scuttled it.

After this, Luckner had more than two hundred 'guests' aboard; his humanity was making the ship a trifle crowded. To resolve the situation, he captured a French four-master, the *Cambronne*. He had the crew take down and destroy its top masts and other rigging to reduce its speed, then put the prisoners on board with the captain of the *Pinmore* in command. The *Sea Eagle* was then able to make its escape long before the disabled *Cambronne* reached land and sounded the alarm.

A LUCKY ESCAPE

By late March 1917, the Royal Navy had had enough of Luckner's antics and decided to set a trap for him. An armed merchant cruiser and two of the navy's armoured cruisers were to lay in wait for the old windjammer before she rounded Cape Horn. But the Sea Devil's luck held. A storm blew Luckner's ship far off course to the south, and it swung into the Pacific and up the Chilean coast unmolested on 18 April. Sailing east of Christmas Island in early May, Luckner learnt of the United States's entry into the war and promptly turned his attention to American shipping. He captured and sank three U.S. vessels in the next ten days.

However, the *Sea Eagle* was now limping. Sailing westward across the Pacific, it reached the French-governed Society Islands, and put into a tiny atoll named Mopelia, five hundred kilometres from Tahiti and the French colonial capital of Papeete, to have its hull scraped of barnacles, which were reducing its speed. Too large to cross the reef, it was anchored outside, and there it was wrecked. Luckner claimed the ship was struck by a tsunami, but American prisoners said the mishap occurred while Luckner and his crew were having a champagne-fuelled picnic on shore.

The crew and prisoners were now stranded on the little island, but they managed to salvage provisions, firearms and two of the *Sea Eagle*'s boats. The daring and indefatigable Luckner now concocted a new scheme. He rigged one of the twelve-metre open boats as a sloop, which he named *Kronprincesszin Cecile* (*Crown Princess Cecile*) and set sail with five of his crew. His optimistic, grandiose plan was to sail to Fiji via the Cook Islands, confiscate another sailing vessel, return to Mopelia to pick up the remainder of his crew and prisoners, and resume raiding.

After a three-day sail, Luckner and his crew landed at Atiu in the Cook Islands, pretending to be Dutch Americans crossing the ocean to win a bet. The gullible New Zealand administrator bought the story and gave them enough supplies to reach another island, Aitutaki. There the administrator was suspicious of their story and odd accents, so Luckner pushed on to the island of Rarotonga. Arriving in the dark, Luckner saw the silhouette of what he thought was a light cruiser (it was actually a beached ship), so he continued west to Fiji, finally landing on the island of Wakaya after a voyage of 3,700 kilometres in an open boat.

The Fijians at first welcomed the 'shipwrecked Norwegian sailors', Luckner's latest cover story, but one sceptic notified Fijian authorities. On 21 September 1917, police arrived and threatened to blast Luckner and his crew with a cannon. Having no taste for bloodshed and not recognising that the cannon was merely ornamental, Luckner surrendered. The New Zealand authorities then confined him to a prisoner-of-war camp on the island of Motuihe, off Auckland, New Zealand.

SOME FAST TALKING

That might have ended the career of the Sea Devil, but Luckner wasn't to be so easily contained. At the camp, he ingratiated himself by admiring, one boat lover to another, the commandant's prize motor launch, the speedy *Pearl*. Three months after being captured, he and fellow prisoners seized the *Pearl* and set out for the Coromandel Peninsula.

'What prisoner does not always dream of escape?', he said. He also dreamed of resuming his raids. At Coromandel he seized a eighty-tonne scow and headed for the uninhabited Kermadec Islands, a thousand kilometres northeast of Auckland. But others had guessed his destination, and Australian and New Zealand naval vessels cornered the escapees there and arrested them. Precisely one year to the day after he set out on his raiding spree, he was in custody. He lived out the war in prisoner-of-war camps in New Zealand before being sent home to Germany in 1919, where he was acclaimed a national hero and awarded the Pour le Mérite, also known as the 'Blue Max', the nation's highest decoration. He spent the rest of his life delivering lectures about his exploits and was reunited with his family, who soon forgave him for not becoming a cavalryman.

French infantry and British troops returning from the front lines together in 1917

The British naval blockade was beginning to smother the German home front, so in February 1917 the Germans resumed unrestricted submarine warfare. This caused the United States to sever diplomatic ties with Germany and, on 6 April, declare war. On the western front, the Germans surreptitiously withdrew to a massively reinforced chain of defences, the so-called Hindenburg Line. Encouraged by the prospect of American support, the Allies geared up for a new joint offensive in April. Despite the horrors of Verdun, France's new commander in chief spoke only of victory and promised his troops that a solution to the stalemate was at hand.

CHAPTER FIFTEEN

ENOUGH ALREADY!

THE FRENCH MUTINIES OF 1917

The infantrymen of the French army had been waiting for this day for more than three months, some of them for as long as three years. At 6 a.m. on 16 April 1917—a grey, rainy morning—they were to launch a massive offensive based on a strategy developed by their recently appointed commander in chief, General Robert Nivelle. The strategy, Nivelle had promised, would finally pierce the German lines and win the war for France within forty-eight hours.

More than one million French soldiers would be involved. The focus of the attack would be the commanding German positions on the heights along the Chemin des Dames, the 'Way of the Ladies', between Soissons and the historic cathedral city of Reims, northeast of Paris. Nivelle's strategy consisted of a gigantic artillery bombardment lasting several days, then 'rolling barrages' that crept steadily forwards. Crack infantry units would follow, but, instead of going over the top in a single vast wave, they would target weak points in the German defences. These spot attacks would surprise and confuse the enemy, and in the turmoil the massed French reserves would push through. The surprise would be enhanced by dividing the bombardment into two stages. After an initial three-day barrage, the Germans would assume that an infantry attack would follow, and would come out of their trenches, but they would then be hit by a second bombardment and the rolling barrages.

Nivelle delivered rousing speeches about the plan, which he had already used with great success at Verdun. There, it had helped French forces recapture the key fortress of Douaumont and push the 'Boche' back to their original lines. It had also won Nivelle his promotion. The attack on the Chemin des Dames would be a triumph, the men were told. The Germans would crumble, and the war would end.

Since December, the men of the infantry, or *poilus* as they were known (a word meaning 'hairy' or 'shaggy'), had been rehearsing their manoeuvres until they could almost perform them in their sleep. They were jubilant. Nivelle's idea appealed to the French devotion to attack, the preferred military strategy since the time of Napoleon. There would be no more struggling to gain just a few metres at a time. At last, there would be a real breakthrough and a final victory.

Typical of the units leading the advance was the Second Battalion of the Eighteenth Regiment. It had been chosen as one of the strike forces because of its reputation as a strong, steady and experienced unit. Many of the men had been together since the Marne. They had fought in some of the western front's major battles. Many had been decorated for valour. They held to a French tradition that dated back to Napoleon's day: unflinching obedience, trust in their officers, faith in their fellow soldiers. Deep down, they understood the need for discipline.

FRUSTRATION TURNS TO HORROR

The morning of 16 April stirred a familiar feeling for the veterans of the Second Battalion and others like them: a mixture of apprehension and uneasiness, as well as a desire to get on with the job. In the cold drizzle, the battalion nervously formed ranks. A sergeant blew his whistle, gave the command and the men moved out to the roar of the guns.

It was not easy going. The terrain was full of shell holes, turned to gooey mud by the rain. Each man was weighed down by twenty-seven kilograms of equipment—Nivelle had been so confident of a rapid advance that he required each man to carry three days' rations. The soldiers slipped and slithered, and lurched from side to side under the weight of their packs. Matching the pace of the rolling barrage proved impossible. The artillery fire was to advance fifty metres every two minutes—far too fast for the overburdened men.

When they reached the tangle of barbed wire in front of the German positions, their frustration turned to horror. The bombardment had failed to cut the wires: barricade after barricade remained intact. As they halted, trying with chilled fingers to cut through the wire or attempting to clamber over it, other troops pressed up behind them. All were now sitting-duck targets. Even worse, the rolling barrage had moved so far ahead that it no longer provided any cover. The Germans were able to emerge from their trenches and rake them with rifle and machine-gun fire. Dozens collapsed on the barbed wire, bleeding and dying.

Somehow, some men managed to advance towards the German trenches despite the enemy fire. The Second Battalion, notably, held together as a more or less cohesive unit. But then fresh German forces burst out in a savage counterattack. The advance broke apart. Men ran in all directions. Many fell. The survivors straggled back behind French lines, some taking two days to get there.

By then, only two hundred of the Second Battalion's original six hundred men were left. All along the Chemin des Dames the story was the same. Estimates had been for between ten and fifteen thousand casualties, but the field hospitals were overwhelmed by ninety thousand on the first day alone. Wounded men had to lie outside the tents in the mud and rain, bleeding, crying and dying. Far from being an end-the-war breakthrough, the much-hyped Nivelle offensive had been a colossal disaster.

Unknown to the men in the ranks, some high-ranking officers, including Nivelle subordinates, had been opposed to the plan. The war minister, General Louis Lyautey, had resigned rather than preside over what he expected to be a disaster. Angry officers now confronted Nivelle at a combative high-command meeting. Nivelle tried to shift the blame, lambasting his underlings for their poor leadership. Outraged, General Joseph Alfred Micheler burst out: 'You wish to make me responsible—me, who never ceased to warn you! Do you know what such an action is called? Well, it is called cowardice!' The other officers watched in embarrassment as Nivelle turned and stumbled from the room, his career over.

Army bulletins continued to claim the advance had been a success. But Paris was only one hundred kilometres away, and the offensive had

General Robert Nivelle

attracted hordes of journalists and politicians, so word of the calamity spread rapidly. Rumours raced through Paris that two hundred thousand had died and another five hundred thousand were wounded. Headquarters refused to issue official casualty figures—long afterwards they were given as 135,000 dead—which only heightened the rising panic.

Cries arose to call off the offensive immediately, but many units and men were still in exposed positions. The Second Battalion of the Eighteenth Regiment, for example, had to keep fighting. As it battled on, it lost almost all of its company commanders and junior officers, its most seasoned sergeants and corporals, and about half its enlisted personnel. In return, it gained, at best, half a kilometre.

Finally, the remnants of the shattered battalion were pulled off to a rest area outside the combat zone. They assumed their numbers would be replenished by new men and officers from the reserve, and they were led to believe that they would soon be transferred to the relatively quiet Alsatian front to regroup. Meanwhile they rested and took solace in their *pinard*, the daily wine ration.

BREAKING POINT

But on 29 April, the Second Battalion sergeants came through the camp with disheartening new orders. There would be no transfer to Alsace. No reserves would be coming: the army—and indeed the country—had run out of men. The battalion survivors were to assemble immediately and march forwards to relieve another exhausted, battle-shattered unit at the front.

The men looked at each other in disbelief. They had just been through hell. They had been promised relief, then made to wait in a so-called 'rest area' that was, in fact, a sea of mud within earshot of the terrifying guns, with virtually nonexistent medical services and hardly a tent or cot to rest in. Their uniforms were in tatters. Some of them had been in the lines for more than a year—despite an official leave policy of four days off every three months. And now they were being told to risk their lives again! Other units hadn't even been in the battle. Why couldn't they go? It was unjust!

Even the veterans began to grumble. 'It isn't fair', a voice cried, perhaps fortified by wine, 'We're not going!' One man took off his pack, set down his rifle, then dropped to the ground. Another man sat down next to him, then a third. Shouting angrily, dozens of soldiers refused to move.

The sergeants had never confronted anything like this. Disobeying orders in the midst of war? Did the men understand what they were doing? The sergeants took little groups aside and quietly warned them: mutiny, disobedience, leaving one's post in the presence of the enemy—these were capital crimes, punishable by a firing squad. They appealed to the soldiers' sense of comradeship: the men in the front lines were exhausted, they desperately needed relief. And where was the troops' patriotism? Their beloved France was in mortal danger. The battalion's few remaining officers tried to help, picking out men they knew and attempting to bring them round. But by then the unit had dissolved into a shouting, howling mob. No one was listening to the officers any more. Even an appeal from the quickly summoned battalion commander didn't help.

Some of the men disappeared into nearby woods. Some moved back to the rest area. Others lay down and slept. Finally, at about 2 a.m., the sergeants managed to assemble a formation of about sixty men. Next morning, stragglers reappeared from the woods. Slowly, the unit re-formed.

But word of the battalion's outright revolt immediately spread through the army. All over France, troops who had endured three years of a seemingly pointless bloodbath said, in effect, 'Enough already!'

Two days after the Second Battalion uprising, the crack Second Colonial Division erupted. Ordered back to the front, the men reported with neither packs nor rifles and flatly refused to move.

Officers of a battalion in the Seventy-Fourth Regiment returned from a reconnaissance to find that four-fifths of the troops had left their posts. The 129th Regiment confronted its commander with demands for more pay, better leave and better food. A unit of the 298th took over the town government in tiny Missy-aux-Bois and declared it would no longer obey military orders, only those of its own 'government'. One mutinous group even commandeered a Paris train, aiming to lay their grievances before the Chamber of Deputies, and were only foiled when military police chopped down trees and laid them across the tracks.

Truckloads of troops careened through encampments, shouting to others, 'Come join us!' and 'Don't go back to the trenches!' Within a month, elements of fifty-four French divisions had rebelled. In some units, nearly half the men were refusing orders. An alarmed headquarters reported to the war minister, Paul Painlevé, that only two reliable divisions stood between the Germans and Paris. Morale was crumbling. Moreover, as the official postal censor reported, soldiers were sounding a new political tone in their letters, which included exhortations such as 'We demand peace!' and 'Revolution!' The soldiers took inspiration from a recent wave of industrial strikes in France, many of which were led by women.

One letter listed the following demands, which had been presented to the commander of the Thirty-Sixth Regiment (the fifth demand was inspired by the fact that colonial troops were being used to keep order in Paris and had fired on female strikers):

1. Peace and the right to leave, which is in arrears.
2. No more butchery; we want liberty.
3. On food [sic], which is shameful.
4. No more injustice.
5. We don't want the blacks in Paris and in other regions mistreating our wives.
6. We need peace to feed our women and children and to be able to give bread to the women and orphans.

WE DEMAND PEACE, PEACE, PEACE!

EVERYBODY WAS DOING IT

After three bloody years of war, men on both sides had had enough. And despite threats of court-martial and execution, they said so, and in turn changed the course of the war.

In February 1917, a garrison of seventeen thousand men in Petrograd (St. Petersburg), the Russian capital, marched through the streets in a protest demonstration. In August, four hundred German sailors marched through the naval-base town of Wilhelmshaven, shouting 'Down with the war!' Seventy-five were imprisoned and their leader was shot. A mutiny forced Bulgaria to cancel an offensive against the Allies at Salonika. Also in the east, ethnic Czech, Hungarian and Slovene units of the Austro-Hungarian army refused to fight.

Even the normally resigned and docile British had their mutiny: at Etaples in France, in September 1917, men who had been hospitalised refused to take part in tough retraining exercises. When military police intervened, the mutineers threw the camp commandant and twelve other officers into a nearby river.

The clinching mutiny occurred on 27 October 1918. Ordered out to sea for one last naval showdown, the German High Seas Fleet five times refused direct orders to leave port. A thousand men were arrested for treason, but the incident forced the kaiser to abdicate, clearing the way for the Armistice.

Military and government leaders blamed pacifist and socialist groups for fomenting the mutiny. One particular target was the 'Bonnet Rouge', the organ of the syndicalist movement which, despite heavy censorship, managed to spread the notion that French labour unions should join with the leaders of the uprisings then going on in Russia and demand an end to the war. Syndicalists were said to meet troops arriving in Paris on leave and urge them to strike; it was even alleged that prostitutes had been enlisted to lure soldiers into joining the mutiny. An embittered General Nivelle claimed that pacifist propaganda had sapped the élan of troops and led to the defeat of his offensive.

THE IRON FIST COMES DOWN

Fortunately for France and its allies, the Germans did not attack during this period of turmoil. They used the lull in fighting to strengthen their defences, but their intelligence failed completely to pick up on what was really going on. The French also succeeded in keeping news of the mutinies from their long-term ally Britain and from the United States, which had recently declared war and was beginning to send troops to France. And despite their protests, the vast majority of soldiers didn't abandon their positions or stop fighting; they simply refused to go on the offensive. Most seemed to regard their actions as a form of strike rather than a mutiny.

The strikers' demands were, however, becoming increasingly extreme. One intercepted letter from a soldier in the 274th Regiment to a member of the Chamber of Deputies read: 'Do not forget that we hold in our hands the destiny of the country. If by this winter you have not shown your willingness to negotiate [with the Germans], we will give way'.

Clearly something had to be done—and quickly, before the Russians pulled out of the war on the eastern front and released countless German divisions for a potentially overwhelming attack. So Nivelle was cashiered, and the job was turned over to Marshal Philippe Pétain, who had commanded the successful defence at Verdun. Pétain had expressed strong reservations about the Nivelle offensive. He favoured a strategic defence, in which the enemy would be confronted by heavily fortified positions and allowed to exhaust itself trying to punch through. His policy would be to hold the line, repel German attacks, and wait for the American troops. There would be no misguided offensives on his watch.

An old infantryman, Pétain was sympathetic to the needs of the men in the ranks. One of his first acts was to notify commanders that they were responsible for seeing that the troops were well fed. He improved the abysmal medical service and insisted that rest areas be outfitted with tents and cots. He decreed a strict policy of four days' leave every three months. He published a booklet entitled *Why We Fight* and had it distributed to troops, and he visited virtually every division.

But Pétain also had to restore order, or all would be lost. Responding to the recent 'collective indiscipline', as the mutinies were officially known, he wielded an iron fist. He ordered that the ringleaders of the mutinies be court-martialled and, when ringleaders could not be identified, that men be pulled from the ranks and tried as examples. In the next weeks, 3,427 men were convicted of offences relating to the mutinies, and 554 were sentenced to death. Only fifty-five were executed, but they included at least twelve shot without trial under orders from overzealous commanders. Soon, Pétain had restored the French army as a fighting force—although it was almost a year before the generals would trust the men enough to launch a full offensive.

The iron fist came down on the Second Battalion six weeks after the uprising. Told to name 'ringleaders', the officers selected twelve men: eleven privates and a Corporal Cronau. He was accused because 'a big, blond corporal' was said to have exhorted the crowd. But when the court-martial began, it was discovered that Cronau had been hospitalised during the disturbances. A substitute corporal was needed. Officers hastily fingered one named Moulia. He was a valiant fighter who had been decorated three times. He was also short and dark, not big and blond. No matter. For the authorities, guilt and innocence were less important than setting an example. Moulia was picked for court-martial.

The process was swift. The accused men were marched into a bleak, spare room in the divisional headquarters to face a frowning panel of officers. A prosecutor quickly presented the case against them, with little positive testimony. Questioned about their role, the defendants claimed that they had not been ringleaders, just part of the crowd. All were immediately found guilty. Six were sentenced to imprisonment in a penal colony. Six others were sentenced to be shot: five privates and Corporal Moulia. The sentences were to be carried out at once.

But as the condemned corporal was being led away, he felt a need to relieve himself. He asked his guard to take him behind a barn. At that very moment, an unexpected barrage of German artillery fire rained down. The guard panicked, and the execution party broke up in confusion. Five prisoners were quickly rounded up, but one leapt over a fence and escaped: the resourceful Corporal Moulia.

It was a clean getaway. No trace of Moulia was ever found. Twenty years after the Armistice, it was reported that he had been spotted in South America. Whether he ever reflected on the mutinies his unit ignited, or the good fortune that freed him, is not known.

Lenin speaking in Petrograd in October 1917. Trotsky is to the right of the podium.

An economic crisis and the continued strain of the war effort fuelled rising discontent in Russia in early 1917. There were regular demonstrations, while groups of workers formed committees, known as Soviets, to elect their own representatives with a view to replacing those in government. In late February, war-weary, food-deprived crowds took to the streets of Petrograd, with cries of 'Bread!' When the Petrograd garrison refused to halt the disorder, the czar was forced to abdicate. A shaky provisional government was established, with the Petrograd Soviet as the dominant force. Observing the turmoil with satisfaction, the German government then played a trump card, hoping to finish off the Russian campaign.

THE LENIN EXPRESS
RUSSIA'S EXIT FROM THE WAR

The train eased gently out of the station, picking up speed as it rolled along the tracks. A trackman waved his lantern amiably as the cars passed, but no answering wave came from within the hurrying train. The coach doors were locked tight, blinds were drawn. No lights escaped from the darkened windows, and the few stragglers on the platform could not see inside.

Within the coach, a short, stocky man with a squarish beard and a fierce stare alternately sat, paced and fulminated to the two women and twenty-five men who accompanied him. His true name was Vladimir Ilich Ulyanov, but he had adopted another name: Lenin. His week-long ride across Europe in April 1917 was to change the course of the war and the tides of history.

THE PRODIGAL SON COMES HOME

The story of the 'sealed train' that whisked the exiled Lenin back to Russia has become the stuff of legend. The passenger list was a Who's Who of the Bolshevik movement in exile, including Lenin's wife, Nadezhda Krupskaya, and Inessa Armand, an energetic and vehement revolutionary, as well as Lev Kamenev, Karl Radek and Grigori Zinoviev. These last three would play a prominent role in the tumultuous events of the next months and die in Stalin's purges of the 1930s. Most of the other travellers were members of the fiercely radical wing of the Social Democratic Labour Party (SDLP), headed back to Russia after years in exile, and chomping at the bit for action now that Czar Nicholas II had given way to a provisional government.

Lenin himself had been sent to Siberia in 1895 and, except for brief interludes, had lived abroad since, most recently in Zurich. A lawyer by training, he had completely dedicated himself to revolutionary causes after the execution of his elder brother for alleged complicity in a plot to assassinate the czar. He had produced a relentless stream of books and polemics exhorting the Russians to overthrow the repressive czarist monarchy and replace it with a workers' government. In 1903, he had helped to organise the Bolshevik wing of the SDLP, and quickly manoeuvred himself into the position of primary leader and string-puller, even while in exile. When war broke out, he became an implacable foe of the Russian monarchy. The war, he said, had nothing to do with the people but was a struggle among capitalist nations for markets, raw material and cheap labour, and all socialists should fight against it.

That kind of rhetoric from a Russian was music to German ears. They wanted nothing so much as to get Russia out of the war, one way or another, so that they could concentrate their armies against the Allies on the western front. At the same time, they were faced with their own breed of radicals, and worried that letting an inflammatory Lenin loose on the world might inflame Germans as well as Russians.

NOW, HERE'S MY PLAN

The train trip was the crafty Lenin's idea. The Russian provisional government that had replaced the czar was composed of squabbling factions, but still supported the war and even pressed for offensive action, notwithstanding army and navy mutinies and peace demonstrations in the ranks. Lenin believed that a hard shove by a strong leader and organised party devoted to revolution would topple the shaky structure, replace it with a workers' party, and take Russia out of the war. With his fiery speeches and intense beliefs, he considered himself the man to do it.

The other Bolsheviks in exile had wanted to return home, too, after the fall of the czar, but they had opted for the traditional route of applying for visas and waiting for approval. Lenin had no time for such legal folderol. He approached the German government head-on, using the secretary of the Swiss Socialist Party, Fritz Platten, as go-between. Platten went to the German legation in Berne, which put him in touch with the German foreign office, which in turn arranged for a Russian émigré, Dr Alexander Helphand, to talk directly to the German high command. Helphand argued before the commander in chief, Erich Ludendorff, that sending Lenin to Russia would mobilise Russian radicals and antiwar groups, and bring pressure on the government to take Russia out of the war. Ludendorff was willing to take the gamble and gave his approval. Kaiser Wilhelm approved, too, seeing a potential dual benefit: it might result in not only bringing the war to an end, but also sideline Lenin and silence his infectious calls for worker revolution in Germany.

Now that he had a German go-ahead, Lenin outlined his terms. He could have returned to Russia via Allied territory, crossing France from Switzerland by train and then travelling to Russia by ship, but he feared that the Allied nations, desperate to keep their shaky ally fighting, might arrest him en route. He could have flown, but the plane might have been shot down. So he requested a train to take him and his party to Sweden, from where they would travel through Finland to Russia. But not a normal, scheduled train. He asked for a train that would cross Germany with extraterritorial rights, making it immune to baggage or passport inspections, like a foreign embassy on wheels. This train would make no stops, and no German official would be allowed to set foot on it. The foreign office agreed to every demand. The sealed train was on its way.

ON BOARD THE SEALED TRAIN

The travelling party first went by train from Zurich to the tiny village of Gottmadingen on the German border. Each paid his or her own fare, as Lenin had insisted. The sealed train was waiting for them. It wasn't much of a train, certainly not luxurious. It consisted of a baggage coach and a single green-sided German Railway second- and third-class passenger coach, divided into eight compartments. The single men occupied the hard wooden third-class benches, leaving the upholstered second-class seats to the women and those travelling with families. There was just one toilet, to be used by all. All external doors were locked, and only Platten, in charge of the trip, was permitted to talk to the guards who accompanied them. A chalk line was drawn between the soldiers' rear compartment and that of the revolutionaries, representing a 'border' between German and Russian territory.

By common consent Lenin and his wife occupied the forward second-class compartment, so that he could work. He spent the journey wrestling with a new formation of Bolshevik doctrine, which he announced to the others en route. Instead of a two-stage takeover of power, the Bolsheviks would now seek a direct and forceful move towards a socialist state.

As Lenin worked, Inessa Armand wrote to her children, whom she had been forced to leave in Russia when sent into exile. The others talked, argued politics, read, sang the 'Marseillaise' and cracked jokes. Several times, an angry Lenin came out of his cabin to quieten them.

The entire trip took nine days, the train following a circuitous route due to the fact that the main lines were reserved for troop movements. It was sidetracked in Berlin for twenty-four hours, then given priority for the rest of its journey, even holding up the train of Crown Prince Wilhelm for two hours. It arrived at Sassnitz on the Baltic Sea on 12 April, where the group boarded a ferry to Sweden, then took an overnight train to Stockholm. After a grandiose welcome from Swedish socialists, they took another train to the Finnish border, traveling the last miles by horse-drawn sledge over the frozen Tornio River.

A RAPTUROUS WELCOME

Fellow Bolsheviks in Russia had been alerted to Lenin's journey, and the word quickly spread through political circles and the government. The provisional government reacted in a way understandable in a society whose government had long been riddled with intrigue and deception: it spread the word that Lenin had sold out to the Germans, that he was carrying bags of gold, and was to serve as a German agent.

The government could have stopped Lenin at the Russian border, but in a fatal lapse of judgment, allowed him to enter, convinced that he would be denounced as a German spy and they would score a major propaganda victory. Instead, Lenin arrived on 16 April to a tumultuous welcome. He was greeted in the ornate private waiting room of the former czar with bouquets of roses, champagne and a brass band.

One of Lenin's first acts was to publish a new tract, *April Theses*, listing all the reasons the provisional government must be brought down and peace sought with Germany. Over the next days, he went from street corner to street corner calling for an end to the war. 'What do you get from war?', he shouted at the crowds. 'Only wounds, starvation and death!'

Despite strident opposition from Lenin and his fellow Bolsheviks, the government, dominated by Alexander Kerensky, chose to launch one more offensive against the Austrians on 18 June. It went spectacularly well at first. Forty-five divisions under General Aleksey Brusilov attacked on a wide front and advanced thirty kilometres on the first day. But then the weary Russian army simply quit. Imbued with revolutionary zeal, many refused to fight. Whole divisions threw down their arms and went home, or simply disappeared. A second attack aimed at German troops was halted and thrown back. Again the Russian army melted away.

Some of Lenin's fellow Bolsheviks then decided that enough was enough. It was time to get the war over with, once and for all. In July, they surreptitiously goaded the Petrograd garrison to rise up and overthrow the provisional government. But Prime Minister Kerensky was still popular. He cracked down hard on the rebels, and a roundup of Bolsheviks followed. Lenin went into hiding again, this time in Finland. But he remained the Bolsheviks' moving spirit.

When the new chief of the general staff, General Lavr Georgievich Kornilov, attempted a coup, marching on the Petrograd Soviet on 25 August in an effort to take power, the troops refused to follow him. Rattled, Kerensky decided to make peace with the Bolsheviks, and Lenin came back to town. The Bolsheviks won majorities in both the Petrograd and Moscow Soviets, the locally elected assemblies of workers, soldiers and tradespeople. Officially, these groups were to 'advise' the provisional government, but because they had directed the strikes and protests that brought down the czar, they had become increasingly powerful. With the Bolsheviks in control of the two largest Soviets in the nation, Kerensky agreed to share power in a five-man directorate. Lenin's colleague, and later military commissar, Leon Trotsky, presided over the constituent assembly of Soviets. The Bolshevik Party called for an All-Russian Congress of Soviets, a gathering of representatives from regional Soviets, to reinforce its position. Before it could be assembled, the troops in

LENIN'S LADIES

The two women in the sealed train both had close ties to Lenin but were quite different in appearance, personality and revolutionary ardour. Nadezhda Krupskaya, known as Nadya, married Lenin in 1898, while both were in exile. A dowdy woman, she was described by the writer Maxim Gorky as 'not very bright' and 'psychologically not very sound'. Although a member of the Bolshevik ladership, she would play only a minor role in the party after returning to Russia.

Inessa Armand, known widely but not publicly as Lenin's mistress, was of very different stock. She was a striking woman, as early photos show, born in Paris to an actor father, but brought up by an aunt in Moscow. She became an idealistic reformer, starting a school for peasant children and a charity to help destitute women. When the czarist government frustrated her causes, she joined the illegal SDLP and was given two years in Siberia for distributing illegal propaganda. On release, she joined the Bolsheviks in Paris, met Lenin, and stayed at his side thereafter. Following her return to Russia, she championed women's causes and chaired the First International Conference of Communist Women in 1920. She died of cholera in 1921, aged forty-six. At her graveside, it is said, a tearful Lenin broke down—the only time he was ever seen to show public emotion.

Petrograd announced they would no longer obey Kerensky's government. 'The Petrograd Soviet is our government', they declared.

Lenin saw his golden opportunity. Without waiting for the congress, he called for immediate revolt. The Soviets poured thousands of their supporters onto the streets, where they were joined by the garrison troops and sailors from the port. In 'ten days that shook the world', the title of the famous sympathetic volume written by American John Reed, the Bolsheviks completely took over the Russian government by shouting down opposition in Parliament and installing their own leadership. On 8 November 1917, Lenin was unanimously acclaimed chairman of the Council of Peoples' Commissars by the Soviet Congress. In one of his first speeches as chairman he called for negotiations on seeking a 'just and democratic peace', without annexation of territories or payment of indemnities. His listeners were ecstatic. 'The war is ended! The war is ended!' they shouted.

PEACE AT ANY PRICE

But ending the war and gaining peace was not that simple. Die-hard Bolsheviks wanted to keep fighting. They hoped that prolonging the fighting would foment revolution among the working class in Germany, already forced to rummage through garbage for scraps of food. Lenin simply rode them down. He immediately approached the German high command to start peace talks. To the alarmed Allies, he simply said, 'We don't want a separate peace. But peace we must have, and if we can't seek it together, the blame is on you.' The people who had brought Lenin to power were demanding an end to the war, and Lenin urgently needed to consolidate Bolshevik control. Peace it had to be.

Leon Trotsky was named chief negotiator. His slogan was 'No War, No Peace', meaning that the hostilities should end without territorial gains or reparations. But the Germans held all the cards. They asked for huge slices of Russian territory. When Trotsky refused, they blithely announced that the war was on again. Lenin sent Trotsky back, telling

Nadezhda Krupskaya in 1930

him, 'Your way has been tried and it has failed. Now it's a question of saving the revolution. You must go back there and sign a treaty of peace.' The humiliating Treaty of Brest-Litovsk was signed on 3 March 1918. It gave Germany everything asked for—and more. In a supplementary agreement approved in August 1918, Lenin's government was forced to pay Germany 120 million rubles in gold for 'reparations' for damage to German property. For the Germans, the outlay on a private train for a crowd of expatriate revolutionaries was recovered many times over.

The Australian Light Horse advancing towards Jerusalem in 1918

British forces were first sent to the Middle East to protect the Suez Canal and to access vital petroleum reserves then under Ottoman control. In Egypt, the British fought off energetic Turkish attacks in February 1915 and August 1916. In Mesopotamia (now Iraq), British forces advanced up the Tigris River during 1915, only to be cornered and forced to surrender at Kut al-Amara in April 1916. By 1917, however, Turkish forces appeared to be weakening and the British went on the offensive, first aiming to take Gaza, the southern gateway to Palestine. But two assaults in March and April failed spectacularly. Clearly, new leadership and innovation were required if lasting gains were to be made.

TRIUMPH OF THE LIGHTHORSEMEN

THE LAST GREAT CAVALRY CHARGE IN HISTORY

The men on horseback came roaring out of the east, shouting, raised bayonets glinting in the desert sun. At the bottom of the long slope ahead rose the minarets and mosques of the ancient biblical city. Crouching in trenches beneath this skyline, the city's defenders watched the approaching riders with awe and bewilderment. This was something few of them had faced before. Surely the riders would soon stop and dismount? Yet still they came on, closer and closer, straight at the lowered guns and machine-gun nests, and apparently oblivious to them. Eight hundred men abreast, they spurred into full gallop as they neared then overwhelmed the trenches. Successful though it was, a charge like this one was seldom seen again. Indeed, some still call it the last great cavalry charge in history.

Prior to World War I, cavalrymen had been the darlings of every army and every old-time commander. They conjured up a classically romantic image of war: gallant mounted soldiers sweeping out of the mist, with their sabres flashing, to put a panicky enemy to rout. It was an image that died quickly on the western front, where battle lines were often only metres apart and machine-guns could literally make mincemeat out of advancing horses and men alike.

In the Middle East, however, with its vast open spaces of level land where Arabian horses and camels had roamed for centuries, it was a different story. There, mounted troops, many of whom had grown up on horseback and trained in the wide, untamed territories of British dominions such as Australia and New Zealand, gave the desert fighting of World War I a different dimension. And the ride of the Australian Light Horse into Turkish positions at Beersheba, on 31 October 1917, matched, for sheer gallantry and effectiveness, almost any of the fabled cavalry charges of the past.

HERE COMES THE BULL
Following the setback of the failed British offensives on Gaza, the British appointed General Edmund Allenby as commander in chief of the Egyptian Expeditionary Force, in June 1917. A cavalryman himself, Allenby had been a successful though not outstanding commander in France. He cut an imposing figure of strength, however. 'A very large and superior general', T. E. Lawrence called him. The troops nick-named him 'the Bull'.

Allenby had been given a simple, succinct mandate: take Jerusalem by Christmas; or, as the new prime minister, David Lloyd George, put it more gently, make the great holy city of Christianity, Islam and Judaism 'a Christmas present to the nation'. Given the lack of progress on the western front, Lloyd George, the British government and the British public badly needed a triumph somewhere. And there was another incentive. The Ottoman Empire was crumbling, and its troops were underfed and becoming demoralised. One last push might just knock the Turks right out of the war. To help ensure victory, Allenby was given one hundred thousand fresh soldiers, most of them from the dominions of the British Commonwealth. The German high command feared a Turkish collapse, too, and eager to keep Turkey in the war, reluctantly agreed to transfer two divisions badly needed in France.

General Edmund Allenby, 'the Bull'

Allenby concluded that the best strategy for capturing Gaza was not by direct assault on its strong and ancient fortifications, as had been tried in the initial British offensives, but by a flank attack on the biblical city of Beersheba, which anchored the eastern end of the Turkish-German defense line, fifty kilometres inland. Beyond Beersheba lay only fiercely hot and desperately parched land. No one, Allenby reasoned, would expect an army to mount an attack from there. There was an added plus to taking Beersheba. The old oasis city was the location of seventeen wells, fabled since Old Testament times, and a potentially life-saving source of water for overstretched desert forces. The key to capturing Beersheba lay with Allenby's mounted men—but not just any such horsemen. Allenby needed riders who could cope with the desert heat and deftly manoeuvre their charges over arid, rocky terrain. Fortunately, he had them in his Desert Mounted Corps and, in particular, among the men of the Australian Light Horse.

ORIGINS OF THE LIGHTHORSEMEN

It was said that in the Australian outback the abillity to ride a horse was as basic as the ability to walk. The roots of the Light Horse went back to the early days of the first British colonies in Australia. In the 1850s, during the Crimean War, local militias and volunteers formed mobile units, variously known as cavalry, yoemanry and mounted rifles. Although they did not fight in Crimea, these units were retained afterwards and became a colonial tradition. Normally they were made up of citizen soldiers who rode their own horses and trained together in their spare time. These weekend warriors were men whose bush life had taught them how to survive for long periods with minimal food and water. After Australia became a federation in 1901, the government organised the mounted units into 'Light Horse' brigades with eighteen regiments apiece. These soldiers were not conventional cavalry but infantry who used horses to take them into battle—hence 'light-horsemen.' By 1914, there were twenty-three Light Horse Brigades, which became part of the Australian Imperial Force (AIF).

Sent to Egypt, the AIF Light Horse did not at first have an easy time. At Gallipoli, two brigades, fighting as dismounted infantry, were ordered to make an early-morning charge across a narrow ridge called the Nek. But the Turks had machine-guns strongly positioned in nine lines of trenches, and the first line was literally cut to pieces. The second line was also decimated, as were two other lines. By day's end there had been 372 casualties, including 235 Light Horse killed.

Back in Egypt after Gallipoli, three brigades of the Light Horse and one of the New Zealand Mounted Rifles were formed into the Anzac Mounted Division, part of the Desert Mounted Corps. They were thrown into battle against the Turkish attack on the Suez Canal in August 1916 and participated in the first attacks on Gaza, where they gained vital experience but continued to fight dismounted and suffer heavy loss of life. For the attack on Gaza, Allenby had four brigades of Light Horse available and he assigned them a critical role in his plan.

A NEAT TRICK

The new offensive began on 31 October 1917 with a series of feints to fool the enemy into believing that yet another major attack would be directed at Gaza. British vessels offshore joined in bombarding the port, as though in preparation for an attack. Allenby also benefitted from some sly counterintelligence. A British agent, Richard Meinertzhagen, had sent several fake, easily interceptable radio messages suggesting that the British would make a frontal assault on Gaza. He had also prepared a fictitious letter, ostensibly from a British officer to his wife, telling her about the plans for the attack. Meinertzhagen put this letter in a dispatch case and rode towards the Turkish lines; then, when attacked, he pretended to be wounded and dropped the case. The Turks took the bait and shifted more forces from Beersheba to Gaza.

Meanwhile, small knots of mounted Anzacs, maintaining strict silence, had stationed themselves in two small oases in the Sinai Desert below Beersheba. The Turks and their German allies were dug into two lines of trenches at the base of a promontory called Tel el-Saba, with supporting trenches protecting their flanks. The night before the offensive, having watered their horses, the Anzacs crept under cover of dark into the hills above the city. As dawn broke on 31 October, and with attention focused on Gaza, horse artillery opened a bombardment, and ninety minutes later, British infantry struck at the entrenched enemy garrison. The Anzacs, along with British units,

LAWRENCE OF ARABIA

Immortalised in literature and film as 'Lawrence of Arabia', Thomas Edward Lawrence was an Oxford graduate and later research fellow, schooled in archaeology. He went to Syria in 1911 on an archaeological expedition and quickly became familiar with and captivated by Arab ways, learning the language and adopting Arab dress. The British recruited him as an intelligence agent and in 1916 he linked up with the Arab Sheik Faisal, then heading a rebellion against Turkish rule. Lawrence began leading Faisal's forces in guerrilla warfare from the Arabian Desert. He succeeded in distracting the Turks just as Allenby was launching his September 1917 offensive, particularly with his daring, unheard-of crossing of the Sinai Desert to take the port of Aqaba. Lawrence and Faisal's rebels then participated with Allenby in the capture of Jerusalem and then Damascus. Lawrence later attended the Versailles treaty talks as a British adviser, but resigned in disgust when he felt the Arabs were being betrayed. He died in a motorcycle accident in 1935.

were to fight dismounted after riding close to the lines. The Third Light Horse Brigade, galloping under heavy fire, got within fifteen hundred metres of the fortifications, then dismounted and pushed slowly forwards. Then the Second Light Horse Brigade advanced at a gallop, again braving heavy fire. They dismounted and sent their horses back—so quickly that the Turks believed they were retreating and fired on the riderless horses. The diversion gave the dismounted Light Horse time to advance unharmed and they rushed the Turkish lines with bayonets drawn. The Turks in the front trench broke, but they then regrouped and mounted a spirited defence, using artillery and machine-gun fire to hold the Allied attack in check.

For the next hour, as the sun sank, the two sides held their positions. The Allies could clearly see the Beersheba mosques, and pick out the location of the important wells. There was even an inviting pond of water shimmering in the afternoon sunlight. It was no mirage but a souvenir of a surprise rainfall a few days before. They could also see that the trenches were not protected by barbed wire.

Lieutenant General Henry Chauvel, commander of the Desert Mounted Corps, knew that his horses—and men—must have water soon or the attack would have to be called off. The only possible solution seemed to be a charge in the classic cavalry style, the sort of bravura display epitomised in Tennyson's 'Charge of the Light Brigade'. But such an advance had not been attempted since the great charge against the Dervishes at Omdurman in the Sudan in 1898 and a cavalry attack against emplaced machine-guns and heavy cannon was almost unheard of. Chauvel had already committed two Light Horse brigades from his reserve. He was loath to risk more. But he still held the Fourth and Twelfth brigades. Brigadier General William Grant, commander of the Fourth, came to Chauvel's headquarters and said his horses were desperate for water. He begged to be allowed to charge, sure it would carry the day. But what should it be? A flank attack, or straight at the guns? When the questions were put to Chauvel, he looked at his staff and commanded in a level voice: 'Put Grant straight at it'.

A CHARGE AT TWILIGHT

With the purple desert twilight approaching, the Fourth and Twelfth brigades assembled behind a protective ridge. They drew up into a charge formation and moved out into the open. They could clearly see their course: a long, slight, barren downward slope leading to the enemy positions almost two kilometres away. The dun-coloured buildings and the minarets of Beersheba loomed above the lines, marking their target.

With the Fourth Brigade on the left and the Twelfth on the right, they came forwards in the traditional three-line charge formation. Horses five metres apart from each other, they first advanced at a walk-march, then a trot, then a canter. A German officer in the trenches surmised that they were preparing to move forward and then fight as dismounted infantry. 'Wait until they dismount, then open fire', he commanded, ordering his artillery to sight their guns on the horses.

But about a kilometre from the enemy lines, the Light Horse suddenly spurred their horses into a gallop and drew their bayonets. Cheering and waving their bayonets, they began to whip their mounts into a faster gallop and made straight for the enemy lines. The Turkish artillery opened fire, but the charging troops were moving so quickly that most of the shells soared harmlessly over their heads. After they had covered another half kilometre, the enemy opened up with rifle and machine-gun fire, but the Allies' supporting artillery soon got the machine-guns' range and silenced them.

Nearing the trenches, the Light Horse pressed their mounts even faster. As the horses thundered towards them, some of the defending troops, unnerved, threw down their arms and fled. The Twelfth Brigade jumped the trenches and their cowering defenders, leaving the Fourth to leap to the ground, plunge into the trenches with bayonets drawn and fight hand to bloody hand. Two squadrons of the Twelfth galloped through the defences and into Beersheba itself—and just in time. Demolition charges had been set to blow up the precious wells and important buildings. Using a captured German demolition officer, the Light Horse disarmed the explosives. By nightfall, Beersheba and its historic wells were in the hands of Allenby's army.

Of the eight hundred men who charged, only thirty-one had been killed and thirty-six wounded. The fall of Beersheba swung the tide of battle towards the Allies definitively. Within a week, they had rolled up the enemy lines and taken Gaza from the rear. Then they moved north, reaching Jerusalem on 9 December—more than two weeks ahead of schedule. Fighting their way beyond Jerusalem against an increasingly weakened Turkish force, and with the Light Horse as their spearhead, they took the last Ottoman bastion of Damascus in October 1918, bringing about a Turkish surrender.

Italian soldiers retreating from Caporetto in October 1917

Italy's declaration of war on Austria-Hungary in May 1915 was motivated partly by a desire to reclaim Italian-speaking realms then held by Austria, most notably in the Tyrol. Accordingly, it attacked Austria-Hungary in the Isonzo River valley in Trentino. By June 1917, Italy had launched ten offensives in the Isonzo, gaining relatively little territory and incurring massive casualties. From the Allied point of view, however, the ongoing campaign could be judged a success in that it pinned down some five hundred thousand Austrian troops.

FIRST FORWARDS, THEN BACKWARDS

HEMINGWAY'S ITALIAN FRONT

The young Ernest Hemingway wanted desperately to fight in World War I. An adventure-seeker from childhood, the Illinois doctor's son tried several times to enlist as soon as he turned eighteen, four months after the United States entered the war in April 1917. But each time he was rejected for poor eyesight, said to be the result of a high-school boxing match. He protested that his hunting exploits proved he could sight a rifle, but the recruiting officer said no. Disappointed, he returned to his job as a cub reporter on the *Kansas City Star*, dutifully turning out obituaries and stories of police arrests while yearning for something more. Then he heard that one of his friends had volunteered as an ambulance driver. That seemed a way to at least get where the action was. He was rejected there, too, on his first try, but on the second go-round the American Red Cross Ambulance Corps accepted him, in December 1917.

Soon, he was on a ship bound for Italy, 'a big, strong, robust, eager, kid more than six feet tall', as one friend described him. Once there, he was assigned to the little-known but savagely fought-over Italian front, which was given short shrift in Allied planning or in newspaper coverage. Hemingway's involvement led to his decoration as a war hero. Furthermore, his subsequent account of one major battle would simultaneously bring notoriety to that neglected front and cement the young man's reputation as a novelist.

A BRUTAL CONFLICT

As 1917 unfolded, the Italian army, under its unflinching martinet of a commander, General Luigi Cadorna, continued to throw itself against the entrenched and heavily fortified Austrian positions. It was a brutal conflict. The violent accompanying artillery bombardments by both sides accounted for sixty per cent more casualties per round fired than the nonstop cannonades of the western front. In the rocky mountain terrain, flying rock fragments and splinters and the resulting rockslides were as great a menace as shells.

In August, the Italians launched their eleventh drive to push through the Isonzo line and this time gained more than nineteen kilometres of Austrian territory—more ground than ever before. In October, pressed by his subordinate, General Luigi Capello, who had commanded the eleventh offensive, Cadorna began gathering his forces for another push. This one, he maintained, would take the Italians

THE WHITE DEATH

Artillery fire often set off landslides in the rocky and snowy Austrian and Italian Alps, not only due to the impact of the shell but also as a result of the concussion and noise of the explosion. Austrian winter troops, learning on the job, soon realised that they could use avalanches as a weapon. By aiming their guns high into the peaks above the Italian positions, they could trigger and even direct avalanches that would roar down on the unsuspecting enemy. Moving almost at the speed of sound, the monster volume of snow would engulf whole battalions of men before they realised it was coming. All too aware of its calamitous potential, Italians called the tactic 'the White Death.'

After the war, controlled avalanches were used worldwide to reduce slide threats to railroads and mountain highways, and in scientific studies of avalanches. Cannon (often fired by military personnel) are still used for avalanche control across Europe and the United States and Canada.

to the gates of Vienna. The overstretched Austro-Hungarian army
was short of manpower, armaments and food, and its government was
weakening. The German leadership reluctantly decided they must prop
up their faltering ally and sent seven hand-picked divisions to the
Italian front. All were experienced mountain troops, including ski
troops, veterans of the vicious fighting against the Russians in the
Carpathian Mountains, and the renowned Bavarian alpine troops,
the *Alpenkorps*. One of its units, the Württemburg Mountain Battalion,
included a company commander named Lieutenant Erwin Rommel,
later to be famous as commander of the World War II *Afrikakorps*.

Cadorna knew in advance of the German build-up, but prepared
to take the offensive nevertheless, spreading his troops unevenly along
the front. Meanwhile, on 24 October, the German-Austrian force,
under German command, probed for a weak spot and found it at a
small mountain village called Caporetto, now Kaborid in Slovenia.
Cadorna, defying the advice of his corps commanders, had left the
Caporetto sector thinly defended.

Preceding the offensive with a gas attack, for which the Italians
were poorly prepared, and following up with a rain of shrapnel, the
Austrian and German units smashed through the village and down the
river valley. Shocked and terrorised, the Italians began a retreat that
would become one of the most famous in history, partly due to its vivid
recounting in Hemingway's acclaimed novel, *A Farewell to Arms*.

PICTURING A GREAT RETREAT

Hemingway, of course, hadn't even made it into the army when
Caporetto was taking place and he wouldn't arrive in Italy until April
1918, when he and his friend Ted Brumback were sent to a small
hospital at Schio, north of Verona, and assigned to carry wounded
from the Trentino battlefront, day and night, along winding roads
skirting precipitous cliffs. But through later conversations with
veterans of the battle and visits to battle sites, he pieced the episode
together, producing what the military historian John Keegan has
termed 'one of the greatest literary evocations of military disaster'.

One remarkable passage in *A Farewell to Arms* describes the approach of
Croatian forces, fighting in the advance guard of the German-Austrian

offensive on Caporetto. The Croatians had a reputation as skilled, relentless and savage fighters, and their mere presence in overwhelming numbers put fear into Italian hearts.

> The wind rose in the night and at three o'clock in the morning with the rain coming in sheets there was a bombardment and the Croatians came over across the mountain meadows and into the front line. They fought in the dark and in the rain and a counter-attack of scared men from the second line drove them back. There was much shelling and rockets in the rain and machine-gun fire and rifle fire all along the line.
>
> The wounded were coming into the post, some were carried on stretchers, some walking and some brought on the backs of men that came across the field. They were wet to the skin and all were scared.

The Croatians quickly punched a hole in the undermanned Italian lines and streamed through. The Italians pulled back, pulled back more, broke apart. Panic set in:

> [The Italian medical officer] said that he had heard at the brigade that the Austrians had broken through the Twenty-Seventh Army Corps up toward Caporetto. There had been a great battle in the north all day.
>
> 'If those bastards let them through we are cooked,' he said.
>
> 'It's Germans that are attacking,' one of the medical officers said. The word German was something to be frightened of. We did not want anything to do with Germans.
>
> 'There are fifteen divisions of Germans,' the medical officer said. 'They have broken through and we will be cut off.'

Whole regiments of Italians began to surrender. Lieutenant Rommel single-handedly captured fifteen hundred Italian soldiers, who threw down their arms and rushed forwards to surrender. Soon the Italian commanders ordered a general retreat, recounted vividly by Hemingway from the perspective of the medical teams: 'The

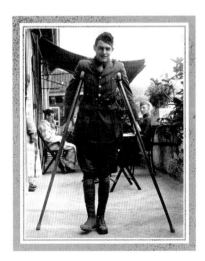

Ernest Hemingway in Milan, in 1918

retreat was orderly, wet and sullen. In the night, going slowly through the crowded roads we passed troops marching under the rain, guns, horses pulling wagons, mules, motor trucks, all moving away from the front'. The retreat was joined by frightened civilians pushing carts loaded with furniture, leading children and driving livestock until it came to a complete standstill in the downpour. Retreating soldiers scattered from the column only to be hit with sniper fire, or shot by their own military police—the ruthless Cadorna had ordered deserters to be shot on sight. But that did not stop whole units from marching into captivity. After twelve fruitless battles on the Isonzo, these exhausted, half-starved soldiers saw an enemy prison as preferable to more hopeless fighting.

Over the next eleven days, the Italians fell back to the Tagliamento River and finally to the Piave. There, having advanced a remarkable 130 kilometres and within sight of Venice, the Austro-German offensive was halted by the river—which was too large and flooded to be crossed en masse—and their dwindling supplies. The Italian losses were about 300,000, of whom 275,000 had been taken prisoner. Just 10,000 or so had been killed or wounded—a very small proportion by the standards of World War I battles. It was one of the worst defeats in military history, and the origin of subsequent jibes about inept and unwilling Italian armies.

A TURN OF THE TIDE

After this, however, Britain and France sent reinforcements and, with their assistance, and American armaments, the Italians held firm through the following months. In June 1918, the Austrians made one more attempt to break through at the Piave. Timed to coincide with a major German offensive in France and with Russia out of the war, it aimed to take control of the northern Italian cities of Venice, Padua and Verona, draw vital Allied forces away from the western front, and perhaps even knock Italy out of the war and seal a final victory for the Central Powers. But the Austro-Hungarian army of June 1918 was very different from the victorious force at Caporetto. Short of food and armaments, and demoralised by news of privation at home, rumours of governmental upheaval, and defection of Czech and Slavic troops, it was a mere shell of its former self. It managed to cross the Piave at night on 15 June and establish a beachhead, but the Italians counterattacked and hemmed the invaders against the river. In a nightmarish effort to recross the Piave, the Austrians lost 150,000 men. Meanwhile, another wing of the army, set on capturing Verona, was counterattacked by combined Italian, British and French units, and suffered forty thousand casualties within a week.

By now Hemingway was in the thick of things. After several months of ambulance driving, he had concluded that the work was too tame and applied for a transfer closer to the battlefront in mid-1918. He was posted to a Red Cross military canteen at Fossalta, on the Piave. It was a place where tired soldiers could come for a cigarette or a cup of tea, to write letters, read, or listen to music. Evenings, after dishing out chocolate or cigarettes all day, Hemingway would hop on his bicycle and pedal out to the front lines, ostensibly to distribute cigarettes or candy but also to witness the fighting and its aftermath and talk to the troops.

On 8 July, he rode forwards as usual. Artillery and mortar fire echoed on both sides. Hemingway—the Italians addressed him as Tenente, since he held an honorary rank of lieutenant—moved from man to man with his offerings, exchanging a few words in his broken Italian. Just after midnight, a shell exploded above him. The force of the explosion knocked him down. Shrapnel tore into his legs. 'It felt like the stings of a hundred wasps', he was to say later. An Italian soldier lay dead next to him. He could hear another soldier wailing in agony. With great effort and pain, Hemingway crawled to the wounded man's side. Despite his wounds, he hoisted the man on his shoulders and began to stagger towards the command post, some 150 metres away. His friend and fellow driver Brumback visited him later and wrote to his parents: 'Ernest, after he had regained consciousness, picked the man up on his back and carried him to the first-aid station. He says he does not remember how he got there, nor that he carried the man, until the next day when an Italian officer told him all about it and said that it had been voted to give him a valour medal for the act.'

There was more to the story, however. When Hemingway was about halfway to the command post, an Austrian machine-gun opened up on him and his burden. Hemingway was hit in the knee and shoulder and went down. Again he struggled to his feet and completed the painful trek to the command post. There he passed out and was transferred to a roofless stable, where he lay surrounded by wounded and dying men. Finally, he was taken by ambulance to an aid station, where he was found to be carrying 227 shell fragments, 27 of which doctors were able to remove before sending him, again by ambulance, to a major hospital in Milan.

Hemingway was hospitalised for three months while the remaining metal was extracted and his wounds were treated. He had to use a wheelchair at first, then crutches, followed by a cane. Meanwhile, he gleaned more about Caporetto from other patients and also met and became infatuated with an American nurse from Pennsylvania, Agnes von Kurowsky. Their relationship is thought to have been the model for the tragic romance in *A Farewell to Arms*, although Ms Kurowsky always denied that a romance had occurred.

As Hemingway was recovering, the Austro-Hungarian army was falling apart. The two defeats on the Piave effectively ended its partici- pation in the war. Negotiations for an armistice began in early October, and on 3 November, Austria-Hungary surrendered. By January 1919, Hemingway would be on his way back to America, proudly bearing his Italian Croce di Guerra, awarded for his actions on 8 July. Once home, he would be acclaimed as a hero and launch his new career as a novelist.

A British tank in action at the battle of Cambrai, November 1917

With the failure of the April 1917 Nivelle offensive and the crisis in the French army, it was left to the British to keep pushing for a breakthrough on the western front. The successful capture of the Messines ridge on 7 June, following the detonation of huge mines under the German positions, offered a glimmer of hope. But the disastrous Third Ypres offensive, also known as Passchendaele, which dragged on from August to November and cost 240,000 casualties for minimal gain, left the Allies in despair. His position increasingly untenable, British commander Sir Douglas Haig decided that the time had come to try a new form of warfare.

CHAPTER NINETEEN

THE COMING
OF THE TANKS

THE ADVENT OF MACHINE WARFARE
ON THE WESTERN FRONT

One grey dawn in November 1917, the men of the German Second Army felt the ground tremble and were shaken awake by a deafening roar. They looked at each other: this was different from the customary pre-attack artillery bombardment. Peering over the parapets of the Hindenburg Line trenches, they were met by a strange and frightening sight. Heading directly towards them came a line of head-high 'mysterious monsters', as the Germans later described them, rumbling and rocking, and ripping easily through the entanglements of barbed wire. 'The devil is coming!' one young man shouted. No one waited to see or hear more. Every one of the soldiers climbed out of the trench and took to his heels, fleeing the unearthly 'devil's coaches'.

Thus came the tanks, which were to change warfare forever. In the next four hours, the inexorable machines, grinding relentlessly along at a mere six kilometres per hour, penetrated eight kilometres deep into the German position near the important rail junction of Cambrai, and carved out a salient eight kilometres wide. They climbed over the Hindenburg Line's trenches with ease, tore out machine-gun nests, and knocked down fortified houses. Behind them came the British infantry. The Germans were so panicked that eight thousand surrendered before noon. The Germans reclaimed much of the captured ground a week later, but a breakthrough had been achieved and the success was such that London church bells rang out for the first time since the start of the war.

THE VISIONARIES

The breakthrough at Cambrai was more than a simple victory for the tanks and the newly formed BEF Tank Corps; it was also a triumph for a small handful of determined visionaries who had early on seen the potential of armed, armoured vehicles and had fought a valiant battle against obstinate opponents in the British high command. There they had been met with constant scepticism. Tanks? What was wrong with cavalry? The gentlemanly way to fight a war was on horseback, with sabres, or at least with foot-soldiers wielding bayonets. That was the way wars had always been won. Motorised vehicles had no role to play.

Not surprisingly, one of the rebellious forward-thinkers was Winston Churchill. As First Lord of the Admiralty, Churchill oversaw the Royal Navy, which, in the early days of the war, was responsible for the Royal Flying Corps, the forerunner of the Royal Air Force. As the Flying Corps' supporting flights over Flanders escalated, many pilots were being shot down or forced to crash-land. New planes could be manufactured, but trained pilots were more difficult to replace. So the navy established the Dunkirk Armoured Car Force in October 1914, consisting of high-wheeled, high-speed (for the time and terrain) Rolls Royce vehicles that could rush to a downed plane and rescue the pilot. The rescue service was initially successful, but the cars were vulnerable to ground fire. So the navy added boilerplate steel to the sides of the cars. When it was pointed out that the open cars were subject to overhead fire from snipers, they added an armoured roof, too.

One of those who saw the potential of the armoured cars was Lieutenant Colonel Ernest Swinton. An up-and-coming engineering officer, Swinton had been assigned to General Headquarters (GHQ) as the army's official spokesman, writing press-releases about the progress of the war. He noticed that the armoured cars worked fine on roads, but bogged down when they had to traverse muddy fields or shell holes, as they often did to pick up wounded airmen. During a visit to the United States, Swinton had seen tractors that travelled on tracks. A rescue vehicle with tractor tracks would be more flexible, and would save more pilots. But Swinton also saw something else. An armoured vehicle propelled by tractor tracks and equipped with firepower could be a devastating weapon. In December 1914, Swinton put his idea on paper and submitted it to Lord Hankey, his superior at the Committee for Imperial Defence. Hankey was intrigued by the idea, and gave it to his staff to follow up, whereupon it promptly languished in the nearest pigeonhole.

ANCESTORS OF THE TANK

An armoured fighting vehicle was hardly a new idea. That Renaissance genius, Leonardo da Vinci, had designed one in the sixteenth century. During the Crimean War in 1855, a steam-powered vehicle was designed, but it, too, was opposed by traditionalists and in any case the war ended before it was developed. A prototype armoured vehicle was displayed in 1851 at Crystal Palace in London, but nothing came of it. In 1903, H. G. Wells published a short story, 'The Land Ironclads', describing a fictional vehicle thirty metres long with huge wheels that would allow it to cross trenches and climb walls. The story attracted attention at the time but was then quickly forgotten.

Swinton was persistent, however. At his urging, Lord Hankey passed the memo on to Churchill, appropriately since the armoured car idea had begun with the navy. Churchill forwarded Swinton's proposal to Prime Minister Herbert Asquith. The hybrid vehicle might overcome trench warfare, he argued. Asquith turned it over to the War Office. The reaction was lukewarm, to say the least. Lord Kitchener, the war minister, dismissed it out of hand. 'An armed caterpillar would immediately be shot up by the guns', he said.

Still, Churchill was a cabinet minister, and with pressure from such high places, something had to be done. The idea went next to Major General von Donop, Master General of Ordnance. Von Donop had opposed the idea from the first, but now grudgingly agreed that a trial should be held in January 1915, using a farm tractor bought from the Caterpillar Tractor company in the United States.

The trial was a disaster for Swinton and his allies. It was conducted in a driving rain over an obstacle course set up by the War Office. The tractor was to pull a truck loaded with more than two tonnes of sandbags to represent the weight of armour and armaments that would be carried into battle. It handily broke through the barbed-wire barrier, but quickly foundered in the thick mud and eventually had to be pulled out. With a smug air of 'we told you so', the War Office declared that the vehicle had failed its trial. Quite clearly, it was an impractical idea and a waste of everyone's time.

But that didn't stop the indomitable Churchill. Using his heft as a minister, he established a 'Landships Committee' headed by the Royal Navy's director of construction. And then entered Albert G. Stern.

Stern was a retired banker without a military or technical background, but he had heard about the proposed machine and the idea appealed to him. He went to Churchill and offered to underwrite the cost of developing and building such a vehicle. He also volunteered to serve as an unpaid administrator. Churchill named him Secretary of the Landships Committee, with the temporary rank of lieutenant, in May 1915. Swinton then called on Stern and they pooled their energies.

Swinton drafted another memo describing how an armoured vehicle could wipe out machine-gun nests. Since the BEF's 1915 spring offensive had been torn apart by machine-guns (which the general staff had once disparaged as useless weapons), GHQ grasped at it and pressed the War Office for a quick go-ahead. In July 1915, a joint naval and military committee was set up to oversee development. Within six weeks, construction had begun on the first British tank, using off-the-shelf hardware. It was nicknamed 'Little Willie', and it worked.

The indomitable Winston Churchill

'Little Willie' was succeeded by 'Big Willie'. It was designed around a revolutionary idea, the brainchild of a navy engineer, W. G. Wilson. Wilson conceived of a loop of tracks that wrapped around the body of the huge vehicle—a design that was to be standard for years to come. Also known affectionately as 'Mother', Big Willie was over ten metres long, two and a half metres high, and two and a half metres wide. It carried a cannon on each side, two machine-gun turrets, and a crew of eight.

The project was conducted in secrecy, and it was important that no news leaked out. Designating it a 'landship' or 'landcruiser' project was too much of a giveaway. So someone suggested 'tank' as a short, descriptive, memorable and ambiguous label, and the name stuck.

THE TANKS' BIG TEST

Big Willie faced its first big test in January 1916. Before a sceptical War Office audience, it passed with flying colours every test prepared for it: climbing a parapet, crossing a trench and moving over dugouts, shell craters, muddy streams and marshes. A few days later it passed a second test; the spectators included Lord Kitchener, David Lloyd George, then minister of munitions, and other ministers. The cabinet ministers went for a ride in the tank and all declared that money would be appropriated to develop and build it. To the elation of Swinton and his team, even King George V had a test ride and pronounced Big Willie a great asset that should be built in great numbers.

But the opposition did not give up that easily. Kitchener was still unconvinced; he saw the tank as a kind of toy that had no place on the battlefield. When Rear Admiral Sir Murray Sueter, the naval officer who had led the Dunkirk Armoured Car Force, commented to Swinton that 'three thousand of these should be ordered at once', a top general angrily burst out, 'What's it got to do with this damned navy man? Who says we want three thousand tanks?' Even after the successful tests and proponents' arguments that hundreds of massed tanks could achieve the long-sought breakthrough in France, the War Office ordered only forty. After Swinton's pleading, the order was increased to one hundred. At Lloyd George's insistence, it was then upped to 150. But that was still far fewer than tank proponents advocated.

Hurry-up construction began, along with training of a hand-picked tank corps. By midsummer the military had most of its hundred tanks, but was still waiting for training to be completed. Swinton wrote a new memorandum, suggesting that the tanks be withheld until they had enough fully manned vehicles for a surprise attack in overwhelming numbers. The BEF commander, Sir Douglas Haig, endorsed the proposal. But then came the battle of the Somme. After that disastrous loss, Haig flip-flopped. He needed tanks now. Even a few tanks, he said, could make the difference in the giant offensive he was planning for fall. Swinton protested. So did Churchill. But two units of fifty tanks each were dispatched to France.

In the new phase of his Somme offensive, in mid-September, Haig ignored Swinton's suggestions. Instead of organising a massed attack, he spread the tanks thinly. Rather than taking the enemy by surprise, he prepared the way with three days of bombardment, which alerted the Germans that an attack was coming. Then the surprise was completely given away when a solitary tank pushed forwards to clean out a pocket of resistance. Still, the effect on the Germans was devastating. Seeing the ponderous machines, even in small numbers, bearing down on them, troops panicked, threw away their weapons, and headed for the rear. Some of the tanks broke down, some were ditched, some were shattered by shellfire. But they led a drive across a ten-kilometre front that drove the Germans back half a kilometre and captured four thousand prisoners.

The tank attack counted as a success in Haig's eyes, but not in those of some of his staff, who felt their resources could be put to better use. When Swinton visited GHQ after the battle, Haig asked that a thousand more tanks be built. But Haig's chief of staff, Lieutenant General Sir Lancelot Kiggell, one of the most vociferous tank opponents, immediately cancelled the order. 'This cancellation came as a thunderbolt', Stern said. He hurried over to Lloyd George, by then the war minister and president of the Army Council. Lloyd George called Sir William Robertson, chief of the Imperial General Staff, on the carpet. The order for one thousand tanks was restored at once.

TRIUMPH AT CAMBRAI

It was a full year, however, before the tanks could finally be employed in sufficient numbers—at the battle of Cambrai in November 1917. There, under the greatest secrecy, 476 tanks with trained crews were assembled. This time there was no massive bombardment to announce the attack. And the ground was ideal for tank warfare as Swinton had described it in his memos: dry, firm, rolling grassland. With the new Tank Corps commander, General Sir Hugh Elles, standing up in the turret of the lead tank, nicknamed 'Hilda', the tanks formed a massed wall directed at a single point. The Germans had never seen anything like it and had no way to combat it. The British rolled them back eight kilometres.

TANKS? GIVE US GUNS!

The French built tanks, too, and by 1918 had one thousand 'Schneider' models, some mounted by seventy-five-millimetre guns. The skeptical Germans built only twenty, however, culminating in a slow-moving monster that weighed forty-five tonnes and required a crew of twelve. Instead, they focused on bigger and better artillery weapons, beginning with the 420-millimetre 'Big Bertha' used against the supposedly impregnable Belgian fortresses at Liège and Namur in August 1914, and climaxing with the long-distance 'Paris Gun'. Tucked into a woods 120 kilometres from the French capital and capable of firing a man-high projectile twenty kilometres into the upper atmosphere at a speed of 0.6 kilometres per second, the Paris Gun was designed not to destroy armies or fortresses, but to terrorise civilians, and at first it succeeded. The first shells fell on early-morning crowds in Paris on 25 March 1918. Five days later, a projectile ripped through the Church of St Gervais during Good Friday services, collapsing the stone pillars onto the kneeling worshippers. Eighty-eight were killed and sixty-eight seriously wounded. However, the French batteries soon located the gun's position and destroyed it, and the last Paris Guns were disabled by July 1918.

Swinton foresaw the army's failure to build on this initial advance. 'I bet the GHQ were just as surprised by our success as the Germans, and quite unready to exploit it', he said. So they were. The cavalry, which was supposed to sweep in and envelop the Germans from the rear, was too far away to do so. The force's early gains were negated.

Nevertheless, the tanks had finally justified their visionaries' faith and had demonstrated their ability to achieve the breakthrough the Allies had long prayed for. They also paved the way for a new form of fighting, effectively ending trench warfare, as World War II was to prove.

After Cambrai, the pro-tank group was finally given credit for its vision. Swinton was promoted to colonel, and Stern, the temporary lieutenant, became a lieutenant colonel. And the success was yet another feather in Churchill's cap.

German soldiers at a field kitchen on the western front

At the end of 1917, the Allies hunkered down to await the promised U.S. reinforcements. The capture of Jerusalem in December was encouraging, but on the western front the Allies continued to suffer heavy losses. The Germans, on the other hand, following the collapse of the Russian campaign on the eastern front, were beginning to transport enormous numbers of battle-hardened troops west to the Hindenburg Line, giving them, at the beginning of 1918, a clear numerical advantage. German commander in chief Erich Ludendorff recognised that time was not on his side. But if he could strike the Allies before the power of America changed the equation, victory might be within his grasp.

CHAPTER TWENTY

A VICTORY PARTY TURNS INTO A HANGOVER

GERMANY'S LAST BID TO WIN THE WAR

At the beginning of 1918, much of Germany was near starvation. Housewives in Berlin poked through garbage seeking tidbits of food. Bread riots swept several cities, often led by striking workers who could not buy enough food to feed their families. Bread was rationed; so was meat, so was sugar. The ever-tightening British naval blockade had cut off supplies of fruits and dairy products once imported from abroad; rail shipments of other foods had been curtailed because the railways were short of manpower, many of their employees having been conscripted into the army. The staple foods were now turnips and cabbage—when you could get them. Entire families lived on turnip soup.

The German armies were somewhat better off, but not much. Their bread ration had recently been cut in half, and they were allowed meat only twice a week. Eggs were a novelty, unless a soldier or mess sergeant could find a willing farmer or a farmer's hen could be kidnapped. Infantrymen used their rifles to hunt dinner; the menu might feature rabbit or rat. The ubiquitous turnip was the cornerstone of the military diet, too. It appeared each morning in a hot drink made from the ground-up vegetable. The blockade had halted the coffee supply.

The German commander in chief, Erich Ludendorff, considered complaints about famine unpatriotic griping. What was important was the stalemated western front, where the armies had been immovably locked for four years. American troops were flooding into France, more

169

THE FULL DINNER PLATE

Before food shortages began to bite and turnips took over in 1917, German soldiers were fed amply. The daily ration list at the beginning of the war allotted each German soldier 750 grams of bread (or biscuits); 340 grams of meat (as much as a large steak), usually sausage; 1.4 kilograms of potatoes or other vegetables, usually dried; the equivalent of half a litre of coffee; plus sugar and salt. The soldiers were also given two cigars, two cigarettes, or pipe tobacco. The British rations were more generous still: 600 grams of fresh or salt meat, 600 grams of bread or biscuits, 100 grams of bacon, 85 grams of cheese, 225 grams of fresh vegetables, salt, pepper and mustard, plus a 100-gram dollop of jam.

The British also received a 'tot of rum'—at least a tablespoonful—daily. The Germans got half a litre of beer, five centilitres of whisky, or a quarter litre of wine. The French were issued the equivalent of almost a litre of wine a day; some saved their rations for a binge later in the week.

Under the unofficial live-and-let-live policy, firing was usually suspended during the enemy's ration distribution; as one soldier observed, 'Shelling during dinner was sure to bring retaliation during your own dinner hour'.

would soon be coming, and American industry was working full tilt to furnish weapons and supplies to his enemies. Unrestricted submarine warfare, which Ludendorff had advocated, had so far failed to choke off the torrent of men or supplies. The German armies were bleeding and its allies were worse; both Austria-Hungary and Turkey were on the point of collapse. On the plus side, however, a million Germans who had been matched up against Russia, and their guns, were available to fight on the western front, and the German railway system had been working overtime moving them from one side of the continent to the other. Ludendorff could now count 192 divisions to the Allies' 178.

Seeking to exploit this advantage, he mapped out a giant offensive that was designed to smash the Allied armies and achieve a final breakthrough. Much like the failed Schlieffen Plan, Ludendorff's new offensive, code-named Operation Michael, would wheel through Flanders, take the Allied armies in flank and rear, and drive straight and unstoppably towards Paris. Victory would come within a few short months—and then no one would grumble about being hungry.

TEN THOUSAND GUNS

The grand spring offensive began on 21 March, along a eighty-kilometre front on the edge of the old Somme battlefield, with an artillery bombardment that shook windows 120 kilometres away across the English Channel. The focus of the initial attack was the city of Amiens, a rail hub much coveted by the Germans and heavily defended by the Allies. Ludendorff had assembled nearly 6,500 guns plus 3,500 trench mortars of different calibres; these were backed up by more than a million rounds of ammunition. After five hours, the shelling ceased and a gas attack began, the gas held close to the ground by the mist. The infantry then moved forwards. Ludendorff had amassed seventy divisions at the centre of the front. Many were composed of seasoned veterans of the Russian campaign, but others were made up of bottom-of-the-barrel, recent draftees, naive seventeen-year-olds and men

German commander in chief Erich Ludendorff

over forty-two: short of manpower, the Germans had extended the age of eligibility. These men were to overwhelm the outnumbered Allies, after which Ludendorff would launch flank attacks, widen the gap and push the BEF all the way back to the English Channel.

On the first day, everything went according to plan. The German armies advanced thirty kilometres over the entire front, and the British force collapsed. By nightfall, the Germans were just eight kilometres from Amiens. Total victory seemed so near at hand that the kaiser declared a 'victory holiday' for German schoolchildren, freeing them from classes to celebrate—although some were too hungry to do much celebrating.

On the second day, the Germans advanced closer to Amiens and widened the breach. The two-day push was the single most rapid advance on any front during the war. Gloomy Allied generals urged that the armies give up Amiens and pull back towards the Seine River to defend Paris. French Marshal Ferdinand Foch, recently named head of a unified command, rallied them with a stirring speech (echoed during World War II by Winston Churchill): 'We must fight them in front of Amiens! We must fight them where we stand now! We must not retreat a single inch!' The French stiffened, dug in and fought off repeated attacks.

THE HUNGRY GERMANS

The Germans dug in, too, but in a different way. The rapid advance through the French countryside had brought them into Allied rear-area supply depots, hastily evacuated by the defenders. The hungry young men who had been living on turnips and black bread suddenly found themselves confronted by the bounty of the well-fed Allies. While 'les Boches' stuffed themselves on French cheeses and sausages, washed down with giant gulps of wine, the advance came to a standstill. 'Entire divisions totally gorged themselves on food and liquor and failed to press the attack forwards', one German general complained.

German troops in the Champagne sector found even greater riches. The famed wineries of Champagne had continued to turn out bubbly despite the war; indeed, some of the finest vintages were made between 1914 and 1918. The wine cellars, dug deep underground into the chalky limestone, resisted bombardment and were so secure that shops, hospitals and schools were set up inside them. A German officer described what happened when the troops discovered this treasure trove on 28 March:

> As soon as I got near I began to see curious sights. Strange figures, which looked very little like soldiers, and certainly showed no signs of advancing, were making their way back out of town. There were men driving cows before them ... others who carried a hen under one arm and a box of notepaper under the other. Men carrying a

bottle of wine under their arm and another one open in their hand ... Men dressed up in comic disguise. Men with top hats on their heads. Men staggering. Men who could hardly walk.

Much of the army was too busy eating and drinking to fight and next day were groggy or hung over. Those who could rouse themselves continued to plunder. Some troops grew rebellious. 'The troops will not fight', a German general of the once-crack Sixth Army told headquarters, 'the offensive must be canceled'.

Ludendorff was forced to acknowledge the standstill and stand down his men. Had the Germans not been tempted by the riches of Champagne, they might have broken through the Allied lines and overwhelmed their opponents. As it was, the setback further undermined a force that was exhausted and unnerved by news of the conditions in Germany, while allowing the Allies to regroup. Ludendorff refused to give up and would launch further unsuccessful offensives over the following months. But the moment had passed. For Germany, the premature celebrations in Champagne marked the beginning of the end.

The day after the British attack on Zeebrugge of 23 April 1918, Kaiser Wilhelm examines the damage

Germany's resumption of submarine attacks on shipping in international waters, on 1 February 1917, had led to the sinking of American merchant ships and helped bring the United States into the war. As hundreds of thousands of U.S. troops travelled across the Atlantic later in the year, their transport ships faced becoming U-boat targets alongside British merchant shipping. With its American lifeline threatened and losing half a million tonnes of shipping a month for much of 1917, the British navy sought to contain the damage by sending heavily armed convoys to escort the vessels and by patrolling the North Atlantic with destroyers and other anti-submarine craft. But this had limited success, and continuing losses to the U-boats in early 1918 made it clear that offensive action was required.

A GLORIOUS FAILURE?

THE DARING BRITISH RAID ON
GERMANY'S SUBMARINE LAIR

It was an audacious plan, the kind that a nation brought up on Sherlock Holmes and cloak-and-dagger thrillers was bound to relish. Its architect, Vice Admiral Roger Keyes, at forty-five the youngest admiral in the British Navy, was known for his daring and love of aggressive action. He had been brooding on Germany's new campaign of unrestricted submarine warfare, which was taking a heavy toll of Allied shipping. Armed escorts were having limited success and finding the subs in the open ocean was almost impossible. So why not take the attack right to the enemy? Instead of hunting out the elusive subs at sea, why not hit them where it would really hurt? Why not strangle them in their home ports, before they could ever get to sea? Or, as the French commander Ferdinand Foch put it, 'close off one of the lairs from which this animal [the submarine fleet] springs'.

In the early days of the war, the opposing armies had engaged in a 'race to the sea', to capture the vital seaports on the Belgian North Sea coast. In October 1914, the Germans had seized Antwerp and the key city of Bruges, which was linked to the ocean at the coastal port of Zeebrugge by a sheltered, thirteen-kilometre canal, deep enough for cruisers and submarines. Control of this port provided Germany with quick access to the North Sea and thence the Atlantic (thus saving prodigious amounts of fuel), and gave it a naval base within 160 kilometres of the British coast. At Bruges, the Germans had built thick concrete submarine shelters impervious to Allied aerial attack or bombardment by naval guns, and installed floating docks and maintenance and supply facilities. On an average day, as many as eighteen submarines and twenty-five destroyers, as well as torpedo boats and other craft, used the canal to reach the Bruges shipyard. Why not, Keyes said, neutralise this vital facility and thereby defang the submarine monster?

A ROYAL FAVOURITE

Keyes was known for unorthodox ideas that sometimes went against the navy's more conservative voices. He had participated in the unsuccessful effort to force open the Dardanelles, and had favoured a second seaborne thrust instead of the landings at Gallipoli. Born in India, the son of an army general, he had enlisted in the navy at age thirteen, and had served on Queen Victoria's yacht, which made him a favourite of the royal family. He had been decorated and promoted for his leadership during the Boxer Rebellion, and been named commander of Britain's first submarine fleet, in 1910.

Keyes was short and slightly built, and officers of more imposing stature sniffed that he didn't look like an admiral. (Neither did Nelson, Keyes supporters said.) After Gallipoli, he was given a plum assignment as commander of the battleship *Centurion* at the fleet's main base at Scapa Flow. To his annoyance he was then switched to a desk job as director of naval planning; but once there he kept urging the navy command to take action against the subs. Soon, Keyes was named admiral of the Dover Patrol, which was charged with the defence of the English Channel, and given the task of tackling the submarine problem.

The navy had previously developed a plan for an attack on Zeebrugge, but had dropped it because it considered it too risky. Keyes resurrected the plan but added some embellishments of his own. He concluded that a direct effort to capture Bruges could not succeed. But he suggested that the submarine base could still be put out of commission by an attack on its only outlet, the canal's opening onto the sea, which lay just 120 kilometres from Dover. Keyes proposed, in effect, bottling the submarines up in their base so that they couldn't get out. The 'cork' in the bottle would be created by sinking concrete-laden ships across the canal mouth. These ships would be taken across the Channel and steered into position by skeleton crews. Meanwhile, the navy would land a diversionary force of Royal Marines and sailors to attack the fortified installation at the canal entrance, known as the Mole. Their mission would be to silence its big guns, overwhelm the guard contingent and then withdraw as soon as the blocking ships had been dropped beneath the waves.

Despite the opposition of some high-ranking officers, the intricate plan was adopted in the fall of 1917. The Royal Marines assembled a strike force of 1,700 men, and a mock-up of the Mole was built in an abandoned chalk pit. Over the next months, a series of rehearsals and practise drills was feverishly conducted. A regiment of infantry was assigned to play the 'enemy', and under Keyes's discerning eye, the assault was acted out, again and again, to the last letter. Keyes gave the plan the code name 'ZO' for Zeebrugge-Ostende (another Belgian North Sea port) and insisted it all be carried out in an atmosphere of absolute secrecy. The men were not told of their destination or objective until two days before the attack.

Even the choice of ships was a dark secret. For the blocking ships, the navy picked out three over-age, coal-burning cruisers which were almost ready for the scrap heap. Keyes decided early that the naval vessels could not transport such a large landing force and still carry out their other duties. So he commandeered two large passenger ferries from the city of Liverpool ferry service, and even provided the cover story: the *Royal Iris* and the *Royal Daffodil*, their erstwhile passengers were told, were being sent to America to transport the American Expeditionary Force to France. Keyes insisted the ferries would be ideal for the Zeebrugge venture because of their large capacity and shallow draft, which would help them to traverse minefields and shallow waters. They had double hulls and were virtually unsinkable, and were built for lurching and bumping against quaysides, which was at the heart of the assault plan. To shield them from the Mole's powerful guns, which would be firing at pointblank range, the ferries were outfitted with special armour.

Keyes then chose an auspicious date for the great assault. The attack would take place just after midnight on 23 April, St George's Day, the festive day of England's patron saint.

THE FLEET SETS SAIL

On the afternoon of 22 April, a seventy-six-vessel flotilla pushed off from Dover, headed for the Belgian coast. It was led by the primary assault warship, the cruiser *Vindictive*, an old coal-burner considered expendable; the troop-laden *Royal Iris* and *Royal Daffodil*; the three old coal-burning cruisers chosen as blocking ships, the *Thetis*, *Intrepid* and *Iphigenia*; and an antiquated submarine, *C5*, which would play a special role. A force of destroyers and cruisers backed them up, with Admiral Keyes on the bridge of the new destroyer *Warwick*.

A covey of small, fast motorboats darted among the larger vessels. These 'speed merchants' were to stand by and pick up the crews after the block ships had been scuttled and to rescue survivors of the attack on the Mole. A further important task for these small craft was to lay a dense smoke screen to conceal the attack vessels. The resourceful Keyes had discovered a naval officer, Commander Brock, whose father headed the Brock Fireworks Company. Brock had developed a new method of producing smoke by injecting chemicals into the exhaust pipes of the motorboats. The chemical used the artificial sweetener saxin, which was in short supply at the time. Nevertheless, the government decreed that all saxin should be diverted to this project.

Vice Admiral Roger Keyes, architect of the raid

English diabetics thus went without sweetener for several weeks.

A minute after midnight, Keyes sent a coded message to all ships: 'St George for England!' Captain Charles Carpenter, commanding the task force from the *Vindictive*, responded: 'And we give the dragon's tail a damned good twist'. The attack was on.

The night was clear and moonless and the sea calm as the task force pushed towards the Belgian coast. The *Vindictive* was making good headway at a respectable rate of speed, as were the blocking ships in its wake.

The launches skittered about, preparing to release the smokescreen, the light wind promising ideal conditions. On the deck of the *Vindictive*, the lead force lay behind armoured barricades, ready to spring across twelve carefully constructed gangplanks that would allow them to stampede onto the Mole and catch the defenders from the rear. There was no sign that the Germans were aware of the impending attack.

With such a carefully designed and detailed plan, something was almost bound to go wrong. As the fleet neared the coast, the wind subtly shifted; choppy swells came up. Soon the vessels that had been hidden by the smoke screen were fully exposed. The batteries on the Mole opened up on the *Vindictive*, by now only one hundred metres away. The cruiser took several damaging hits as it limped towards its target. Meanwhile, however, the captains of the three blocking ships managed to manoeuvre them across the mouth of the canal. The scuttling operation began and the ships, with their massive load of concrete, began to sink towards the bottom. The crews dived overboard and swam towards the waiting launches.

Things were going less well on the Mole. The assault party's attempt to take the Mole's defenders from the rear had been thwarted by swells and shellfire, which had forced the *Vindictive* ashore one hundred metres short of the planned position, and compelled the attackers to mount a frontal assault, under savage fire, instead. Worse yet, the grappling irons which were to fasten the *Vindictive* to the dock failed to hold. The alert captain of the *Royal Daffodil* nosed his ferry against the *Vindictive* to hold it in place. His effort was successful, but the manoeuvre, combined with the limited number of gangplanks, prevented some of the marines from reaching the battle. Moreover, the *Vindictive*'s guns, which were to cover the landing party, were too low to train on the Mole's deck, and the only cover for the assault party came from a machine-gun mounted on the damaged superstructure.

The marines had also lost several leading officers in the first wave, one of them the English rugby star Arthur Harrison, who had been knocked overboard by a bursting shell and drowned despite the heroic efforts of a petty officer to save him. Not surprisingly, the first attack was repulsed without the marines reaching the big guns. But Commander Brock rallied the remaining troops for a second attack, which was underway as a huge explosion echoed across the port. The old British submarine *C5* had been guided under a viaduct that linked the Mole to the mainland and was the fastest means of access for German reinforcements. The blast destroyed the viaduct, cutting off the Mole. Now isolated, the Mole's defenders withdrew to their blockhouse.

Just after that the *Royal Daffodil*'s whistle sounded the Morse sign 'K'. That was the signal that the blocking ships had been successfully sunk and that the troops should end the attack and return to the ferries. It was supposed to have been sounded by Captain Carpenter on the *Vindictive*, but the cruiser had been badly damaged, losing much of its superstructure, including its communication facilities.

Then came one final setback: as the troops were loading onto the ferries, congratulating themselves on the mission's success and certain they were now on the way home, a German shell tore through the *Royal Daffodil*'s main deck and into the passenger cabin below. Seventy-five marines were killed instantly and another twenty-eight died afterwards.

Carpenter held the *Vindictive* at the dock for an extra ten minutes to load the wounded. Then the fleet headed back to Dover. The attack had taken an hour and ten minutes. All told, 161 of the British force had been killed, 383 wounded and 16 were missing. Thirteen had been taken prisoner on the Mole.

WHO WON? WHO LOST?

The fleet arrived in Dover just before 8 a.m. to a tumultuous welcome. Families were cheering at the dock; other vessels fired their guns and blew their whistles in salute. A message from King George V to Keyes was waiting: 'I most heartily congratulate you and the forces under your command who carried out last night's operation with such success. The splendid gallantry displayed under exceptionally hazardous circumstances fills me with pride and admiration.' Eight of the British, including Keyes, received the Victoria Cross, the empire's highest decoration, for their part in the lightning strike.

The battle wasn't quite over, though. Both sides claimed victory. Kaiser Wilhelm, who had been visiting troops in Belgium, claimed the attack had been repulsed and gave his troops medals all around. The Germans acknowledged that the blocking ships had temporarily bottled up the canal, but said their naval engineers had been able to cut a new channel around the ships within three weeks of the attack.

The British displayed aerial photos of the blocking ships in place, and said twenty submarines and a number of torpedo boats had been trapped in the Bruges shipyard. Other submarines had been forced to detour to other facilities, or to travel on the surface, where they were more vulnerable to attack. Whatever the long-term impact, everyone on the Allied side declared that it was the kind of daring raid in which the British could take justifiable pride.

CALLING THE DEAD

As U-boat attacks sent ships to the bottom with all hands, and young soldiers disappeared into the glutinous mud of Flanders or were dismembered by bombardment, bereft families often desperately sought one more word or touch from their vanished loved ones. Many sought to fulfil this objective through spiritualism.

Spiritualism promised to put those at home in communication with the spirits of the departed in the world beyond. The aggrieved assembled in a darkened room where a 'medium', considered to have transcendental powers, called out to the spirits and then asked them to respond to questions with rapping sounds—one rap for 'yes', two raps for 'no'. Many sorrowing families went away convinced that they had indeed communicated with the lost young men. Others felt they were victims of a hoax.

Spiritualism had sprung from the Second Great Religious Awakening of the 1820s and 1830s, which stressed more direct communication between worshippers and God, as well as with the souls of the departed, and for some time seances had been a common, sometimes playful practice in Britain, particularly among the middle classes. After the disaster of the Somme, however, the practice grew rapidly in popularity, though it declined again with the end of the war. Among the most prominent spiritualists were Sir Douglas Haig, a devoted churchgoer who believed higher powers spoke directly to him, and Sir Arthur Conan Doyle, creator of Sherlock Holmes, who had lost a son in the war, and taught spiritualist practices until his death.

A group of German World War I soldiers including Adolf Hitler (back row, second right)

As the spring of 1918 unfolded, German commander Ludendorff persevered with his offensives, throwing every available man into battle on the western front. In April, Operation George unleashed eight hundred thousand German troops across the old, torn-up terrain around Passchendaele, pushing the British backwards and alarming the Allied command. But the attack collapsed after two weeks of fierce fighting, the British managing to employ tanks and machine-guns to devastating effect. Another desperate German thrust, Georgette, was followed by the Matz offensive in early June, which took the Germans to within eighty kilometres of Paris. But by then disillusion and disorder were spreading through the German army, to the dismay of its most dedicated soldiers.

DRESS REHEARSAL

ADOLF HITLER'S FIRST WORLD WAR

T he young German with the handlebar moustache was a good
soldier, and a brave one, but by the standards of the trenches,
a most unusual one. He neither smoked nor drank, and even
lectured his mates about the dangers of these habits. He never joined the
raunchy dugout conversations about French females. He obeyed orders
to the letter, spoke respectfully of and to officers and became angry when
others groused about the higher-ups. He was cool under fire, seemed
sometimes to be almost courting danger. He spoke little, read a lot,
but sporadically would burst out with torrents of vituperation about
communists, politicians, cowards on the home front and, especially,
Jews, all of whom he claimed were fattening on the war and undermining
the nation. With the failure of Germany's offensives in the spring of
1918, his diatribes became even more forceful and bitter.

Two decades after World War I, this man's fierce resentment would
fuel another global conflagration. The soldier's name was Adolf Hitler.

THE STARVING ARTIST

As most people know, Hitler was not really from Germany. He was born
and grew up in German-speaking Austria, across the border. Although
he preached the cause of pan-Germany, a unification of both states, he
railed against the Hapsburg Empire and its polyglot and, as he saw it,
primitive population. (Slavs and Hungarians actually outnumbered

German-speaking Austrians in prewar Austria-Hungary.) After his parents died, Hitler migrated to Vienna in 1909 and lived hand-to-mouth as a would-be artist, sleeping behind the railway station and reading inflammatory political tracts in the library. After twice being rejected for Vienna's Academy of Fine Arts, he turned to painting postcards and street scenes and selling them, but finally concluded that stodgy old Vienna was stifling to his talent and moved to the more invigorating atmosphere of Munich. And then the war came.

Hitler the soon-to-be warrior actually moved from Austria to Germany as a draft dodger. He was supposed to have reported for service in the Austro-Hungarian army in 1910, and when he skipped town, police were looking for him. Conscription authorities later caught up with him, but he was twice rejected for poor health. In any case, he had no wish to serve the decaying Hapsburg Empire. But Germany! That was another matter. Germany was the pinnacle of world culture and of racial purity, home to what he already considered a master race.

Following the declaration of war, he tried to enlist but was turned down because he was not a citizen. On 10 August 1914, he wrote a personal appeal to King Ludwig of Bavaria, the German state of which Munich was capital, asking to be admitted to the army; to support his case, he described his devotion to the German cause. Nine days later, he was sworn into the First Company of the Sixth Bavarian Reserve Infantry Regiment, named the 'List Regiment' for its commander, Colonel Julius List. With less than six weeks' training, the 'Listers', now part of Prince Rupprecht's Sixth Army, were transported to Flanders and thrown into battle against British forces in the First Battle of Ypres. Their baptism of fire came after the famous Massacre of the Innocents, when twenty-five thousand German greenhorn volunteers straight from universities were slaughtered by the trained British regulars' coordinated and super-accurate rifle and machine-gun fire. The Bavarians were similarly sent against professionals from Britain's Black Watch and Coldstream Guards and were also decimated. They even lost their commander, Colonel List. In his first battle, Hitler proved himself a good soldier, however. He was calm amid the devastating rifle fire, obeyed orders unquestioningly and never lost his nerve. As a result, he was promoted to lance corporal after just three months of service.

THE FAVOURITE MESSENGER FALLS

As First Ypres raged on, Hitler proved himself again. Stumbling across a wounded officer left in the open, he recruited a friend and the two managed to pull the man to safety. Hitler was rewarded with an Iron Cross, Second Class. By then, he was a *meldeganger*, or dispatch runner, carrying messages from headquarters and staff to and from commanders in the field. It was a dangerous assignment, an almost suicidal task that involved dashing through the fighting, often under heavy artillery barrage, yet he had coveted and volunteered for it. It was an important job and one that enhanced his reputation for bravery amid his trench-mates. In the eyes of his comrades, he gained a kind of a halo: for it seemed that anyone who could repeatedly race across a bullet-laced landscape without being wounded must be watched over from above. Hitler did nothing to dissuade believers.

A few months after First Ypres, what was left of the List Regiment was shattered at the battle of Neuve Chapelle on 10 March 1915. The three days of fighting cost the Germans nearly three thousand killed, wounded and missing. Despite repeated narrow escapes and his own willingness to court danger, Hitler was not among them. He was 'as cunning as a fox who knows exactly when to keep his head down', a fellow runner said. At the Somme in 1916, however, he was not so lucky.

Hitler's List Regiment was held in reserve during the early fighting on the Somme, but was shifted to the battlefront in early October to relieve other units. On unfamiliar terrain, the Listers suffered mightily, none more than the dispatch runners. 'A nightmare', one of Hitler's fellow runners said later. Hampered by a loss of leadership, the torn-up terrain and ignorance of the territory, the runners repeatedly became lost. Hitler tried to buoy up the others' spirits with paeans to the nobility of their cause, and emerged as their leader. Hence the unit suffered a severe blow to its morale when he was seriously wounded.

He had taken a piece of shrapnel in the upper left thigh and was lying in a shell hole in a pool of his own blood. Stretcher-bearers reached him and carried him back to headquarters. Hitler insisted that the commanding officer's 'favourite messenger', as he was known in the unit, was not seriously hurt and could go back to his duties. Instead he was evacuated to a hospital-recuperation unit outside Berlin.

It was the first time Hitler had been back in the 'Fatherland' in more then two years and at first he was exultant. He had never visited Berlin, and as soon as he could walk, he requested time to see the capital city. He was agog at the opportunity, but the longer he stayed, the more agitated he became. 'Clearly there was misery everywhere', he wrote later. 'The big city was suffering from hunger. Discontent was great.' Worse was the griping and criticism of the war in the soldiers' homes. 'Scoundrels were intentionally frequenting these places to spread their views,' he said. His favourite city, Munich, was even worse. Sent to a replacement battalion there, he found 'anger, discontent, cursing wherever you went ... To be a slacker passed almost as a sign of higher wisdom, while loyal steadfastness was considered a symptom of inner weakness and narrow-mindedness'.

BIG NAMES OF THE FUTURE

The roster of young men who served, fought and built reputations between 1914 and 1918 reads like a latter-day Who's Who of politics, the military, the arts and history. Hitler's World War II second-in-command, Field Marshal Hermann Goering, was a World War I air ace credited with twenty-two kills. Kemal Ataturk, later the architect of the modern secular Turkish state, commanded a Turkish division at Gallipoli. Charles de Gaulle was captured and imprisoned in World War I; in World War II he led the Free French fighters after his country's surrender and subsequently became prime minister and, later, president of France. Captain Harry S. Truman commanded an artillery battery in France before becoming senator, vice president and president of the United States. Douglas MacArthur won a Congressional Medal of Honor in France in 1918, and later led Allied forces in the Pacific in World War II. The philosopher Ludwig Wittgenstein served in the Austro-Hungarian army, along with the famed violinist Fritz Kreisler. And the two men who led Britain and America during World War II had naval roles in World War I: Winston Churchill was British First Lord of the Admiralty and Franklin D. Roosevelt U.S. Under Secretary of the Navy.

Then there were the Jews: 'The offices were filled with Jews. Nearly every clerk was a Jew and every Jew was a clerk. I could not help but compare them with their rare representatives at the front ... The spider was slowly beginning to suck the blood out of the peoples' pores.' Others on the home front were failing to support the war, too. Workers were on strike, people were protesting the war's course, 'cowards and traitors' were everywhere. 'I could not tolerate the squabble among peoples of the German race', Hitler recalled. The betrayal by civilians became the main target of his invective and would later shape his entire political agenda.

TURNING TO POLITICS

Hitler soon begged to be relieved of 'light duty' and sent back to the front. In February 1917, he returned to his old unit, to his mates' great surprise. The remaining Listers fought in the great struggles at Arras and Passchendaele, and Hitler was decorated for bravery with the Military Cross Third Class with Swords. In March 1918, when Germany launched its grand spring offensive, Hitler welcomed it, sure that victory was within the nation's grasp. Even in June, with German morale declining, Hitler remained confident. When German forces came within sight of Paris, he began planning a triumphant sightseeing tour of the French capital.

But by now American troops were being thrown into combat and their numbers, freshness and vigour were beginning to tell. Gradually and steadily, the German war machine was pushed back towards its own borders. As the grand offensive crumbled, Hitler received an Iron Cross First Class for 'personal bravery and general merit'—recommended, ironically, by a Jewish officer. He continued to fight hard—and condemn the 'cowards and traitors' at home who were, as he saw it, undermining his comrades. But he saw that the cause was almost lost. 'The poison of the hinterland has begun to be effective', he wrote.

Hitler's war would end following a gas attack near Ypres on 13 October. Blinded and unable to walk, he would be evacuated to a military hospital at Pasewalk, near Stettin. There he would hear the news that he had long dreaded, of Germany's surrender—'the greatest villainy of the century,' he later wrote in *Mein Kampf*. And there his career as a lance corporal would end and, with dire consequences for the world, his political career begin.

American troops arriving at Le Havre, France, in 1918

The United States had been far from prepared when it declared war on Germany in 6 April 1917. It had only a tiny army, just 150,000 strong, with virtually no combat experience; no air force to speak of in spite of its early role in aviation; and enormous industrial strength but little of it directed towards war. Nonetheless, the nation began to call on its resources of men and materials, sending an advance American Expeditionary Force to France in June 1917 and launching conscription aimed at mustering an army of three million men. British navy convoys succeeded in protecting American transport ships and by spring 1918, more than three hundred thousand U.S. troops were in Europe, some of them fighting in unconventional roles.

HELLFIGHTERS
OF HARLEM

FRANCE'S BLACK AMERICAN HEROES

It was 2:30 a.m. on a dreary May night in 1918 and the two young men in the muddy and isolated forward position were sleepy as well as nervous. Members of a small detachment of four privates and a corporal, they were stationed in front of the main trenches, and their assignment was to scout for Germans who might creep in under cover of darkness to throw a grenade or drop over the parapet and whisk away a prisoner for questioning. All five of what was called Combat Group 25 had been on duty for three days and nights. Two privates and the corporal were so exhausted that they had retreated to an underground bunker to sleep. Privates Needham Roberts and Henry Johnson were alone.

Suddenly, Roberts heard a click-click sound, which could mean that someone had snipped the flimsy barbed wire around the position. A flare was set off, illuminating the scene with its bright light, and a cry of 'Corporal of the Guard!' went up. Before Roberts could even raise his rifle, he saw a dark figure leap over the parapet. Within seconds, more followed. Roberts raised the rifle and inserted a cartridge clip, which jammed. In desperation, he began swinging the weapon like a baseball bat. He felt the sickening crunch as the rifle stock hit human flesh and bone. But before he could swing again, another dark shape threw a hand grenade into the position, then another. Roberts and Johnson were both knocked down and wounded by the explosions, which also brought down huge chunks of earth and timbers, trapping the three men sleeping in the bunker.

Roberts had managed to get off three shots before the rifle jammed and believed he had hit three men. But he had been struck by shrapnel and a bullet in the shoulder. With his uninjured hand, however, he was able to toss grenades to Johnson, who had picked himself up after the blast and begun to fight back, throwing grenades over the parapet and fighting hand-to-hand with the figures who had jumped into the trench. Close-in rifle fire hit Johnson in the side and in the shoulder. Like Roberts, he began to use his rifle like a club, and 'banged them on the dome real good'. One was armed with what appeared to be a Luger. He must be an officer, Johnson thought, come to capture and question a prisoner. He clubbed the man to the ground, then turned to help his buddy Roberts. Two Germans were trying to drag Roberts away, probably to take him prisoner. Like some other men in the trenches, Johnson carried a long, double-edged bolo knife. Over 180 centimetres tall, Johnson brought the knife down with all his strength on one of the Germans, swinging with such force that he split the man's skull. The officer crawled to his feet and fired his Luger. Johnson fell to his knees with a loud groan, pretending to be grievously wounded. When the officer came over to finish him off, Johnson rammed the bolo into the man's abdomen. 'I disembowelled him,' he said afterwards. The other Germans fled, leaving Roberts but taking their wounded with them.

At daybreak, a relief unit arrived. They found Johnson and Roberts seriously wounded, carrying bullets and shrapnel, and also freed the trio buried in the bunker. They counted four German dead and estimated from the trails of blood leading away from the position that the pair had killed or wounded as many as a dozen more. Newspapers inflated the estimate to thirty and acclaimed Roberts and Johnson bona fide American heroes.

But Needham Roberts and Henry Johnson were not fighting with the American army, but under the French flag. And they looked and spoke differently from the American 'doughboys' then pouring into France, who typically had lily-white faces and regional accents. For these bona fide American heroes had come off the streets and out of the slums of New York—and they were black.

WHATEVER WERE THEY THINKING?

In January 1917, when it appeared that America might join the Allies, German Foreign Minister Alfred Zimmermann had an idea, and convinced the kaiser it was a stroke of genius. He sent a coded telegram to the German ambassador in Mexico City suggesting that if Mexico joined the Central Powers and attacked the United States, 'with Germany's generous financial support', after victory they would be given Texas, Arizona and New Mexico—territories Mexico had ceded to the United States after the Mexican–American War in 1848. The Germans were seemingly unaware that Mexico had only a ragtag army with ancient weapons and that General Pershing had pushed them around easily on a punitive expedition after Mexican bandits crossed the border into a New Mexico town. Or that the country's treasury was empty and Mexico wanted nothing so much as a quiet U.S. border.

On Zimmermann's instructions, the German ambassador in Washington wired Berlin for fifty thousand dollars to influence key members of Congress to cast their ballots against war, if the matter came to a vote. Intrepid British cryptographers decoded both of these messages and informed Washington, releasing the full text of the telegram. Confronted with the flagrant 'Zimmermann telegram' and the Germans' resurrection of unrestricted submarine attacks, President Woodrow Wilson broke off diplomatic relations with Germany and two months later the U.S. declared war.

'LAFAYETTE, WE ARE HERE!'

The triumphant exclamation of 'Lafayette, we are here!' was famously made at the time of the arrival of the U.S. First Division—the 'Big Red One'—in France in July 1917. A reference to the dashing French nobleman who had come across the ocean to lead American colonials in their fight against British rule, it is often erroneously attributed to General John J. Pershing, the ramrod-straight commander of the American Expeditionary Force, though it was actually spoken by Colonel E. C. Stanton, Pershing's adjutant and 'designated orator', at a ceremony at Lafayette's tomb.

Pershing had promised the French tanks, bombs and planes, none of which he had. All he had was men. And the First Division represented the only professional force the United States had when it boldly declared war in April. Even then, they had to borrow rifles and seventy-five-millimetre howitzers from their hosts.

Roberts and Johnson arrived in a different guise. They were National Guardsmen, organised into the Fifteenth New York Infantry Regiment. African-American leaders in New York had recruited the unit, insisting that blacks were citizens, too, and had every right and duty to serve their country. Discrimination by race was constitutionally outlawed, but there was plenty of opposition to arming blacks and training them as soldiers. Might they not rise up, rebel and point their rifles at whites? The opposition was quelled, somewhat, when the regiment was staffed by white officers, most of them upper-class bluebloods with Ivy League educations. Roberts and Johnson's company commander was the upper-crust Hamilton Fish, the son of a Republican congressman, who would later serve in Congress himself.

Pershing, backed by Congress, had insisted from the first that an American army must fight as a unit, under American command. It was not to be dribbled away, man by man or unit by unit, to fill holes in the depleted French or British ranks. French commander Ferdinand Foch and Sir Douglas Haig, his British counterpart, fumed and pleaded, while Pershing stuck to his guns. But he relented a little to allow his greenhorns to be schooled in the tricks and tactics of trench warfare. Not one American, including Pershing himself, had any real-life experience with artillery bombardments or poison gas. Then, when Foch begged for men in the face of Ludendorff's grand 1918 spring offensive, Pershing agreed to 'lend' five divisions to serve with the

Needham Roberts

French army, provided they were kept together and fought together. One of the units was the Fifteenth New York, now officially mobilised into the U.S. Army and renamed the 369th Infantry. The men called themselves 'the Harlem Hellfighters'.

THE EAGER VOLUNTEERS
Roberts and Johnson were typical of the assortment who rallied to the Hellfighter ranks. Roberts, the son of a minister, had grown up in Trenton, New Jersey, which he described as a 'Northern outpost of the Old Confederacy'. Sixteen years old when America declared war, he wanted to lie about his age and enlist, but his parents wouldn't hear of it. So he took the money they had given him to pay their poll tax and bought a rail ticket to New York. There he managed to convince authorities that he was eligible. Johnson was a porter in Albany's Union Station when he heard about the Fifteenth and immediately went to New York and signed up. Other Hellfighters had been shoeshine boys, drugstore clerks, bellhops, cooks, waiters. The regimental bandleader was James Reese Europe, who was musical director for the dancing couple Vernon and Irene Castle, and had written musical plays and revues for them.

As the 369th (the men in the ranks continued to refer to it as 'the Old Fifteenth'), they were sent south to heavily segregated Spartanburg, South Carolina, and ran not into Southern hospitality but Southern hostility. On the streets, the uniformed troops were jeered at; with the Civil War not that far behind them, South Carolinians worried that their own black majority population might be incited to rebel against the segregated system. Those raised in unsegregated New York constantly transgressed the back-of-the-bus and for-whites-only rules, resulting in continual conflict with white officialdom. The unit was confined to base to prevent racially motivated incidents. Finally, Captain Fish and other officers convinced higher-ups to transfer the 369th and continue training in the more hospitable clime of New Jersey.

By late 1917, what had begun as a mere trickle of American soldiers to France became a flood, and 'the Old Fifteenth' was part of it. But in Europe, too, it met hostility. Black soldiers? Blacks were not fit for combat. They were meant for labour, the kind slaves had performed in the cotton fields. (This military attitude still prevailed in 1945, when African-Americans drafted with the author were immediately shunted to the Quartermaster Corps to lift boxes in warehouses.) Accordingly, men who thought they had come to France to fight Germans found themselves working as stevedores on the French docks, unloading ammunition and military supplies.

The regimental officers pressed to have the unit reassigned to combat duty. Captain Fish enlisted his congressman father to carry the case to the war department. The prominent actor E. H. Sothern wrote a letter to the *New York Herald* in support. The regimental band went on tour around France, introducing French audiences to African-American jazz (the French boggled at the band's syncopated version of 'Le Marseillaise'), partly to call attention to the unit. Thirty-seven days into the tour, it was announced that the tour was over. The 369th was headed for the front lines on 12 March 1918.

They were assigned to what the French called *L'Afrique*, colonial units of Moroccans, Algerians, Tunisians and Senegalese. Indeed, the French tended to regard the Americans as Senegalese who spoke English. The 369th was issued French Lebel rifles and French bayonets, and trained with the French Chauchat machine-gun. They ate French rations and received the standard quart (almost a litre) of wine a day (which white officers quickly eliminated). They learnt to respond to artillery bombardment and to gas. After a week of such schooling, the French gave them their own trench to defend.

It was a quiet sector at first; Ludendorff's offensive had paused for breath in May. The men were stationed in the Champagne region, on the edge of the Argonne Forest (known to the Hellfighters as the 'Oregon Forest'). Ludendorff was expected to attack again here, as it was considered the gateway to Paris. Meanwhile, both sides conducted probing operations to fathom the other's intentions. Needham Roberts and Henry Johnson were in the forefront of that effort.

The tactic called for establishing a platoon-sized ambush position ahead of the main line of trenches, with the aim of intercepting any German raiding party. Behind the ambush position were entrenchments and dugouts protected by barbed wire, which were to serve as back-up if any Germans slipped through. These positions were manned by between five and a dozen men, and it was in one of these

Henry Johnson

positions that Combat Group 25 was assigned and Roberts and Johnson proved themselves heroes.

THE RETURNING HEROES

The two men had been evacuated and hospitalised by the time the Germans advanced again in June. The 369th Infantry remained attached to the French army as the fresh American units arrived to bolster the Allies. By July, the United States had half a million men in France and more were on their way. On 18 July, the Allies began a counter-push that drove the Germans backwards, and on 8 August, which Ludendorff afterwards called 'the Black Day of the German Army', they forced the Germans right back to the Hindenburg Line.

American troops then fought in a series of battles whose names would become familiar to generations of American history students—Meuse-Argonne, Chateau-Thierry, Belleau Wood, St Mihiel—along with statements like Marine Captain Lloyd Wilson's response at Belleau Wood when ordered to retreat: 'Retreat? Hell, we just got here!' Men of the 369th fought in all of these battles, as did the 28th Pennsylvania Keystone Division and the 42nd Rainbow Division, so named because of its diversity, its men coming from every American ethnic group.

After the war, the entire three-thousand-man 369th Regiment would be awarded the French Croix de Guerre and return to a heroes' welcome in New York. Joining a ticker-tape parade of U.S. forces in February 1919, they would march up Broadway and Fifth Avenue, stepping to the drumbeat of James Europe's regimental band, and detour through Harlem to the roars of the crowd. And the loudest cheers of all would be reserved for the two men at the head of the parade: Needham Roberts and Henry Johnson.

Soldiers and civilians celebrate the declaration of the Armistice on 11 November 1918

After the Allied counteroffensive in August and September 1918, the Central Powers began to implode. Bulgaria sued for peace on 29 September. Following its defeat at Megiddo, Palestine, on 21 September, Turkey sought an armistice, signed on 30 October. Karl I, the new emperor of Austria–Hungary, wrote to American president Woodrow Wilson on 1 October seeking a truce, and on 3 October the German government followed suit. Yugoslavia, Poland, Czechoslovakia and Hungary asserted their independence. On the eleventh day of the eleventh month of 1918, the guns finally fell silent. The larger political issues of territorial claims, disarmament and reparations would be resolved the following year with the Treaty of Versailles. In the interim, victors and vanquished faced huge economic and human losses. Vast tracts of Europe had been laid to waste, governments had fallen, new nations been born. Almost nine million men had died and twenty million had been wounded. Germany confronted hyperinflation, America a wave of jobless veterans. And even before the war ended, it became clear that another, yet more deadly threat to life had emerged.

THE ENEMY NEITHER SIDE SAW COMING

HOW EVERYONE LOST TO THE 'SPANISH FLU'

In September 1918, the United States's most prestigious pathologist, Dr William Henry Welch, was summoned by Surgeon General William Gorgas to Camp Devens (now Fort Devens), Massachusetts. He and a blue-ribbon team of forensic experts were asked to investigate a mysterious illness that had struck thousands of soldiers about to be sent to France. In the words of one physician, 'bodies were piled up like cordwood' outside the autopsy room. When Dr Welch performed his first autopsy, on a nineteen-year-old soldier, he was aghast at the young victim's purplish, devastated lungs. 'Gentlemen', he told the others solemnly, 'I believe we are facing a new infection. Or a new plague.'

That 'new plague' was to sweep the world and in a few short months kill twenty million people—far more than were killed in the four years of conflict. People called it 'the purple death' because the victims often turned, in one doctor's description, 'blue as huckleberries' as their lungs haemorrhaged. Officially, it was called 'Spanish influenza', because the first official reports came from Spain, which had reported eight million cases in February and March 1918, including that of King Alfonso XIII, but the 'flu' had apparently been carried there by ships originating in the Middle East, after it had jumped from animals to humans. Regardless of origin, no nation and no army escaped its effects.

Flu halted promising offensives by the Allies and Central Powers alike. Ludendorff, always quick to divert blame, claimed the pandemic, not worn-out troops, failures of strategy, or lack of supplies, halted his spring campaign. By the first week of October 1918, forty-six per cent of the French army was sick. The same week, the American commander General Pershing asked for more troops following the U.S. victory at St Mihiel, only to be told that no healthy men were available.

IT STARTS WITH A HEADACHE
The flu was considered a normal visitor almost everywhere, as it still is. People expected—even accepted—a few days of misery, including a few deaths among the very young and the very old. So when the first European cases turned up in the spring of 1918, no one was terribly alarmed, particularly because they were only slightly more numerous and lethal than normal. But as the disease spread and began to fell ostensibly healthy young people, its ravages could no longer be minimised.

The French ports of Brest and Bordeaux, where troopships and supply ships were landing, were particularly hard-hit. The epidemic quickly spread among other troops and into the civilian population and across the ocean. Transatlantic shipping seemed to be carrying it both ways. The first American cases occurred at Camp Funston, Kansas (now Fort Riley), in May 1918, and leapfrogged through the civilian population. Then, as mysteriously as it had arrived, the flu disappeared on both sides of the Atlantic. Armies and civilians breathed a sigh of relief.

But it was as if it had merely taken a summer vacation. The flu returned in September—with a vengeance. The origins of this outbreak were uncertain; the disease seemed to be suddenly everywhere at once. American and British forces sent to Archangel in Arctic Russia to bolster pro-czarist forces in the Russian civil war transmitted it to the civilian population; within a few weeks, ten thousand people in Archangel were ill. In Hamburg, Germany, people died at the rate of seventy-five a day. The disease did not discriminate between rich and poor; when Pershing wired Lloyd George about the St Mihiel victory, the flu-stricken British prime minister responded: 'The news came to me on my sickbed. It was better and infinitely more palatable than any physic.'

Whole military units were decimated. At Camp Devens, previously healthy young men began to line up for sick call by the hundreds, then thousands. By the time Dr Welch arrived at Devens, half the forty-five

A MOST DEADLY FOE

Serbia was the first country into the war, and the first forced out of it—by disease. In 1915, the country was struck by an epidemic of typhus. Carried by the Rickettsia bacillus and transmitted to humans through the bite of a flea or body louse, typhus is characterised by high fever, chills and a virulent body rash. The epidemic felled half the Serbian army, which became too weak to repel the combined Bulgarian and Austrian invasion of 1915. Driven over the mountains into Albania, two hundred thousand soldiers and civilians were evacuated by sea to the island of Corfu. The ill and wounded went to an adjoining island, Vido, where most died and which became known as 'the Island of Death'. A total of two hundred thousand Serbs, military and civilian, succumbed in the mountains or on Vido within a few months. Ultimately, sixty-five per cent of Serbia's total military casualties were due to illness, mainly typhus, and the horrific civilian toll from all causes was estimated at 650,000.

thousand men there were ill—young men who, a short time before, had been pronounced in peak physical health. They complained of chills, headache, fatigue, pain from head to foot, and fevers as high as 40 degrees Celsius. Some dropped dead while waiting to be examined.

Ordinary flu sometimes develops into pneumonia. The air sacs in the lungs, where carbon-dioxide-rich blood is exchanged for the oxygenated variety, become inflamed. Breathing is difficult and laboured. That was what Dr Welch saw in his first autopsy—and in every subsequent one. The air sacs were leaking blood into the lungs, filling them with fluid. The young men were literally drowning in their own blood.

Soon the disease spread to Boston's civilian population, then beyond. Military and civilian hospitals alike appealed for help, but there was none to be had. The epidemic moved south and west, advancing 160 kilometres a day. New York caught the flu, then Philadelphia. Of all the flu-ravaged American cities, the 'City of Brotherly Love' was hit hardest. More than three per cent of the city's one and a half million residents died within a few weeks. At the peak of the epidemic, three hundred Philadelphians were dying of flu each day. More than half a million others were sick.

In Europe the toll mounted rapidly. Britain reported 13,202 deaths from flu in the first week of October, plus another 701 from pneumonia. Over the rest of the month, 35,000 more Britons died of flu and another 2,700 of pneumonia. Paris was hit soon after; 1,500 died in a week, then 3,475 of flu and 1,099 of pneumonia during the remainder of October, and 3,900 more in November. In some rural areas of Europe and North America, whole towns were practically wiped out. The epidemic jumped to India, probably imported by returning troops, causing an estimated seven million deaths there eventually.

No one was immune. Lenin became sick, so did the French prime minister, Paul Painlevé. The artist Egon Schiele and his entire family died in Vienna. The poet Apollinaire died in Paris.

A NEW KIND OF VICTIM

Unlike previous flu epidemics, in which the very young and the very old were the chief victims, the 1918 epidemic hit young adults hardest, particularly those in the thirty to forty age group, people in the prime of life, many with young families. As a result, it created a whole generation of orphans. Large numbers of men in all armies were in the vulnerable age group, and their vulnerability was increased by their close quarters, poor hygiene, bad diet and lack of medical care. Some units quickly lost half their strength; survivors were often to weak to hold a rifle or man a trench. The only compensation was that the enemy got sick, too.

In 1918, no one had even heard of a virus, let alone identified one, so no one knew what had caused the flu, how to treat it, or how to stop it. There were a thousand explanations and a thousand home remedies, plus a handful of conspiracy theories. The flu was said to be a German plot. Those crafty scientists at Bayer, a German firm, had injected flu germs into aspirin, it was claimed, so that if you tried to cure a head-ache, you got flu. That 'explained' why people who were hospitalised got sicker. As the rumour spread, the U.S. government persuaded Bayer to conduct a public experiment to disprove it. Mothers at home sent their sons red peppers to slice and eat; the peppers were said to burn out coughs, colds and fever. Alternatively, they told them to sprinkle sulphur in their boots to protect against infection.

At Devens, doctors hung bedsheets between patients' beds in a vain effort to stop the spread of the infection. Some American troops in France took to wearing gas masks at night, or covering their nose and mouth with cloth to avoid inhaling germs. Other troops were advised to keep their feet dry in the trenches, to drink plenty of water and have regular bowel movements. No one could come up with better advice. Doctors were not only at a loss, but had their own problems. Whole medical teams became ill. Often there was no one to bury the dead.

Then, in the waning weeks of the war, the flu began to disappear. There were fewer and fewer cases, and more and more men were deemed fit to return to the ranks. Just as mysteriously as it arrived, it began to vanish without so much as a fare-thee-well or explanation. On the home front there was a blip when the Armistice was signed and people poured into the streets and hugged strangers in celebration.

But although the armies had put down their weapons, the flu had not entirely abated. It emerged again in January 1919 among fresh U.S. troops travelling to Europe, and the convalescent beds that had

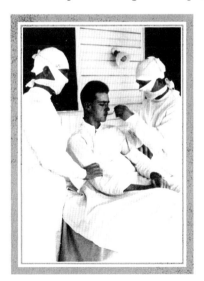

been taken down had to be put up again. In miserable Germany and Austria-Hungary, the new casualties were coupled with an absence of treatment. Simultaneously, the pandemic spread to Australia, where it claimed one hundred thousand lives; to Africa, where an estimated two million died; and to remote areas such as Alaska and South Pacific—one-quarter of the Samoan population succumbed.

By February 1919, however, the flu was a thing of the past, like the war itself. And like the war, no one was able to explain exactly why it had happened.

An influenza patient in a U.S. naval hospital

BIBLIOGRAPHY

Albertini, Luigi. *The Origins of the First World War*. London: Oxford, 1952.

Ashworth, Tony. *Trench Warfare 1914–1918: The Live and Let Live System*. New York: Holmes and Mercer, 1980.

Blond, Georges. *La Marne*. Paris: Presses de la Cité, 1962.

Bowen, Ezra, and the editors of Time-Life Books. *Knights of the Air*. Alexandria, Virginia: Time-Life Books, 1980.

Brook-Shepherd, Gordon. *Archduke of Sarajevo: The Romance and Tragedy of Franz Ferdinand of Austria*. Boston: Little, Brown, 1984.

Brown, Malcolm. *Tommy Goes to War*. London: J. M. Dent, 1978.

Crosby, Alfred W. *America's Forgotten Pandemic*. Cambridge: Cambridge University Press, 1989.

Dedijer, Vladimir. *The Road to Sarajevo*. London: Macgibbon & Kee, 1967.

Dolden, A. Stuart. *Cannon Fodder: An Infantryman's Life on the Western Front, 1914–18*. Poole, Dorset: Blandford Press, New York; distributed by Sterling Pub. Co., 1980.

Doughty, Robert. *A Pyrrhic Victory: French Strategy and Operations in the Great War*. Cambridge, Massachusetts: Belknap Press of Harvard University Press, 2005.

Ferguson, Niall. *The Pity of War*. New York: Basic Books, 1999.

Fromkin, David. *Europe's Last Summer*. New York: Alfred A. Knopf, 2004.

Fussell, Paul. *The Great War and Modern Memory*. New York: Oxford University Press, 1975.

Giddings, Robert. *The War Poets*. New York: Orion Books, 1988.

Gilbert, Martin. *The First World War: A Complete History*. New York: Henry Holt, 1994.

Graves, Robert. *Lawrence and the Arabs*. New York: Paragon House, 1991.

Harris, Bill. *The Hellfighters of Harlem: African-American Soldiers Who Fought for the Right to Fight for Their Country*. New York: Carroll & Graf Publishers, 2002.

Hemingway, Ernest. *A Farewell to Arms*. New York: Scribner, 1926.

Heyman, Neil M. *Daily Life During World War I*. Westport, Connecticut: Greenwood Press, 2002.

Higham, Robin and Dennis E. Showalter (eds). *Researching World War I: A Handbook*. Westport, Connecticut: Greenwood Press, 2003.

Keegan, John (ed.). *The Book of War*. New York: Viking, 1999.

Keegan, John. *The First World War*. New York: Alfred A. Knopf, 1999.

Keegan, John. *An Illustrated History of the First World War*. New York: Alfred A. Knopf, 2001.

Kiester, Jr., Edwin. 'Drowning in Their Own Blood', *PittMed Magazine*, January 2003.

Laffin, John. *British Butchers and Bunglers of the First World War*. Phoenix Mill, UK: Alan Sutton Publishing, 1988.

Lawrence, Joseph Douglas. *Fighting Soldier: The AEF in 1918*. Boulder, Colorado: Colorado Associated University Press, 1985.

Lécluse, Henri de. *Comrades-in-Arms: The World War I Memoir of Captain Henri de Lécluse, Comte de Trévoëdal*. Kent, Ohio: Kent State University Press, 1998.

Lettow-Vorbeck, General Paul Emil von. *Meine Erinnerungen aus Ostafrika (English East African Campaigns)*. New York: R. Speller, 1957.

Macdonald, Lyn. *To the Last Man: Spring 1918*. New York: Carroll & Graf, 1999.

MacKenzie, David. *'Black Hand' on Trial: Salonika 1917*. Boulder, Colorado: Eastern European Monographs, 1995; distributed by Columbia University Press.

MacKenzie, David. *Exoneration of the Black Hand*. Boulder, Colorado: Eastern European Monographs, 1995; distributed by Columbia University Press.

Magee, Frank J. 'Transporting a Navy Through the Jungles of Africa in Wartime', *National Geographic Magazine*, October 1922.

Marshall, S. L. A. *American Heritage History of World War I*. New York: Random House, 1962.

McLean, Roderick R. *Royalty and Diplomacy, 1890–1914*. Cambridge: Cambridge University Press, 2001.

Miller, Charles. *Battle for the Bundu: The First World War in East Africa*. New York: Macmillan, 1974.

Moorehead, Alan. *Gallipoli*. New York: Harper, 1956.

Mosier, John. *The Myth of the Great War: A New Military History of World War I*. New York: HarperCollins, 2001.

Neiberg, Michael S. *Fighting the Great War: A Global History*. Cambridge, Massachusetts: Harvard University Press, 2005.

Oughton, Frederick. *The Aces*. New York: Putnam, 1960.

Palmer, Svetlana and Sarah Wallis (eds). *Intimate Voices from the First World War*. New York: William Morrow, 2003.

Paschall, Rod. *The Defeat of Imperial Germany, 1917–1918*. New York: Da Capo Press, 1994.

Pearson, Michael. *Inessa, Lenin's Mistress*. New York: Random House, 2001.

Pearson, Michael. *The Sealed Train*. New York: Putnam, 1988.

Persico, Joseph E. *Eleventh Month, Eleventh Day, Eleventh Hour. Armistice Day 1918*. New York: Random House, 2004.

Pétain, Philippe. *Verdun*. New York: Dial Press, 1930.

Platt, Frank C. *Great Battles of World War I: In the Air*. New York: Weathervane Books, 1966.

Potter, C. W. 'A History of Influenza', *Journal of Applied Microbiology*, Vol. 91, Issue 4.

Rosenhainer, Ernst. *Forward March!: Memoirs of a German Officer*. Shippensburg, Pennsylvania: White Mane Books, 2000.

Slotkin, Richard. *Lost Battalions: The Great War and the Crisis of American Nationality*. New York: Henry Holt, 2005.

Smith, Leonard V. *Between Mutiny and Obedience*. New Jersey: Princeton University Press, 1994.

Spears, Sir Edward. *Liaison 1914: A Narrative of the Great Retreat*. London: Cassell, 2000.

Steward, T. G. *Buffalo Soldiers: The Colored Regulars in the United States Army*. Amherst, New York: Humanity Books, 2003.

Strachan, Hew. *The First World War*. New York: Viking, 2004.

Taylor, A. J. P. *The First World War: An Illustrated History*. New York: Putnam, 1964.

Thomas, Lowell. *Count Luckner, The Sea Devil*. Garden City, New York: Doubleday, Page & Co., 1927.

Tuchman, Barbara Wertheim. *The Guns of August*. New York: Ballantine Books, 1994.

Watt, Richard M. *Dare Call It Treason*. New York: Simon and Schuster, 1967.

Weintraub, Stanley. *Silent Night: The Story of the World War I Christmas Truce*. New York: Free Press, 2001.

Williams, Charles. *Pétain: How the Hero of France Became a Convicted Traitor and Changed the Course of History*. New York: Palgrave Macmillan, 2005.

Willmott, H. P. *World War I*. New York: DK Publishing, 2003.

ACKNOWLEDGMENTS

First, my thanks to the gifted and creative publisher, William Kiester, who conceived the brilliant idea of publishing this book and asked me to write it. I would say this even if he were not a close relative. And to the extremely talented editor Scott Forbes, whose editorial guidance and contributions are reflected on every page. Thanks, too, to Sarah Odgers for her superb design concept and cover, and to Cathy Campbell for laying out the pages so elegantly. I'm also grateful to the helpful librarians and staff at the Carnegie Library of Pittsburgh, the University of Pittsburgh Hillman Library, the C. C. Mellor Library of Edgewood, Pennsylvania, and the City of Sydney Library and the New South Wales State Library in Sydney. The World War I historians Dennis Showalter of Colorado College and Leonard Smith of Oberlin were generous in discussing their work, evaluating my ideas, and suggesting other sources. Merete (Didi) Hall of Farnham, England, as always, was our helpful source on matters German, as were Jochen and Katja Breitwieser.

My talented wife, collaborator, researcher, adviser, and severest but most perceptive critic, Sally Valente Kiester, Ed.D., waded through many volumes of World War I history and became herself an expert on the gruesome hostilities of 1914–18.

PICTURE CREDITS

Accrington Pals [www.pals.org.uk]: p.90 photograph by kind courtesy of David Bent

Australian War Memorial: Cover photo EO1237, p.8 EO1237, p.64 H10362, p.66 J06392, p.86 H08519, p.102 H12479, p.107 H12425, p.126 H09361, p.144 B01619, p.168 H13220, p.188 H09400

Corbis: p.157, p.192, p.195

Getty Images: p.10, p.14, p.20, p.25, p.32, p.36, p.40, p.46, p.51, p.54, p.75, p.94, p.99, p.110, p.123, p.130, p.136, p.143, p.146, p.152, p.160, p.164, p.171, p.178, p.182, p.196, p.201

Imperial War Museum: p.70, p.78, p.83, p.114, p.118, p.174

Wikipedia: p.43 (Joachim v. Kürenberg, Russlands Weg nach Tannenberg (Berlin: Büchergilde Gutenberg, 1934))

World War I Photos [www.wwiphotos.com]: p.61

INDEX